pocket
cornwall

CW00386398

Wildflowers of Cornwall
and the Isles of Scilly

David Chapman

Alison Hodge

First published in 2008 by
Alison Hodge, 1a Gwavas Road, Newlyn,
Penzance, Cornwall TR18 5LZ, UK
www.alisonhodgepublishers.co.uk
info@alison-hodge.co.uk

Reprinted 2010, 2013, 2017

ISBN-13 978-0-906720-64-6

British Library Cataloguing-in-Publication Data

A catalogue record for this book is available from
the British Library.

Designed and originated in-house

 Printed by Cambrian Printers on FSC Mix

Title page: Thrift

Contents

Introduction

Cornwall and the Isles of Scilly are home to some of the best displays of wildflowers in the world. Just think for a moment about the magnificent bluebells that provide carpets of blue in woodlands such as Lanhydrock and Enys in the spring. At the same time, on the coast we have a scattering of cowslips on the dunes, and cushions of thrift bedecking the already wondrous cliffs of the county – try Bedruthan Steps, or White Island on the Isles of Scilly, for some of our best displays. Among the thrift are many other species of flower which add to the spectacle, and after it has finished there are many others to take its place.

In June we have orchids, some shaped like bees, others like butterflies, but all colourful and shapely – Sylvia's Meadow is among the best locations for these. By the end of June the arable fields come alive with colour. Poppies and corn marigolds are just two of the species which thrive at West Pentire, while Boscregan plays host to the brilliant colour combination of purple viper's bugloss and corn marigolds.

Late summer and early autumn bring a few local specialities, including Cornish heath (on the Lizard), autumn squill and autumn lady's tresses, but the overriding spectacle of colour in this season is provided by our fantastic heathland with the pinks and yellow of heathers and western gorse. For the very best locations head for the Lizard, St Agnes Beacon, West Penwith, or St Martin's on the Isles of Scilly.

Whatever your level of interest in our flowers, it isn't possible to be unmoved by their beauty whether singly or *en masse*, and I hope that this book will help you to get the best out of your experiences with this section of our natural history throughout Cornwall and the Isles of Scilly.

David Chapman
2008

Corn marigolds at West Pentire

About this Book

I have written this book to help introduce a wide range of people living in, or visiting, the county to the wealth of wildflowers that can be seen here. My aim has been to produce a book which is more useful and accessible than most specialist flower identification books through:

- Including only those flowers that can be seen in Cornwall
- Eliminating all but the most essential specialist language
- Suggesting places to go to see the most interesting species
- Noting 'confusion species', where appropriate, and highlighting the key features to help identify them.

In Cornwall and the Isles of Scilly there are about 1,600 species or subspecies of flowering plant, but many of these are obscure, very rare species or subspecies, unidentifiable without the use of a magnifying glass. Given that in a book of this size it hasn't been possible to include all of them, my selection of over 300 species is based on covering the most common varieties, as well as representing a good cross-section of the different flower families and all of those very special 'Cornish' plants.

The species are arranged in the way that is adopted by most botanical books. That begins with the most primitive flowers and ends with the most advanced. In this way, flowers which may be confused are usually grouped together because they are in the same families of species.

Within the text for each of the species in this book I have included:

- The common name and any alternative commonly used names
- The scientific name
- The range of heights, or lengths, that can be achieved by the plant, in centimetres
- The size of the individual flowers, or in some cases the head of flowers, in centimetres (it should be noted that this varies considerably, and plants growing on the coast tend to be much shorter than the same ones inland)
- The flowering season of the plant,

which gives every month in which flowers can be recorded
- A description of the plant, which includes stature, flower, leaf, habitat and distribution
- A list of confusion species including identification features to look for
- For some of the more interesting species I have expanded on the text and included further photographs.

Towards the back of the book (pages 91–3) is a section examining some of the more noteworthy alien species which have escaped from gardens, though we must accept that many of the flowers in the main part of this book are also 'naturalized' species.

Bluebell wood at Lanhydrock

Stinging Nettle
Urtica dioica
Height: 40–160 cm
Flower: 0.1 cm, Jun–Sep
A patch-forming, erect plant with stinging leaves and stems. Tiny flowers with male and female on separate plants, hanging in long thin clusters. Heart-shaped leaves with toothed edges. Grows mostly on waste ground, but also in hedges and on roadsides. Common throughout in suitable habitat.

Confusion plant: none.

Mistletoe
Viscum album
Height: 20–80 cm
Flower: 0.1–0.2 cm, Mar–May
An evergreen plant which parasitises trees such as apple. The many branches hang from the host plant in clumps, and it has distinctive, sticky, white berries. The flowers are tiny and yellowish-green. The tough, yellowish-green leaves occur in pairs and are oval in shape. Grows mostly in orchards, but can occur on some other trees. Uncommon, probably the best location is the orchard at Cotehele.

Confusion plant: none.

Redshank
Persicaria maculosa
Height: 20–80 cm
Flower: 0.1–0.2 cm, May–Oct
An erect plant with a reddish-tinged, hairless stem. The pale pink flowers are tiny but packed in heads which gather into a flower spike. Leaves are long and narrow. Habitat: arable fields. Common throughout in suitable habitat.

Confusion plant: none.

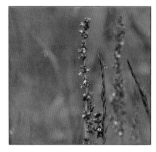

Sorrel
Rumex acetosa
Height: 10–80 cm
Flower: 0.1–0.2 cm, May–Aug
Erect, with thin stem; leaves taste acidic. Tiny red or green flowers; male and female occur on separate plants; flowers borne in thin, almost leafless spikes. The slightly fleshy leaves are spear-shaped, the basal lobes pointing backwards towards the stem. Habitat: grassland, woodland and hedges. Common throughout in suitable habitat.

Confusion plants: some species of dock, though sorrel is much less substantial; Sheep's Sorrel, *Rumex acetosella*, has spear-shaped leaves whose basal lobes point forwards, towards the tip of the leaf.

Black Bindweed
Fallopia convolvulus
Height: 10–100 cm
Flower: 0.1–0.2 cm, Jun–Oct
Scrambling and climbing plant, twining clockwise around stems. Greenish-pink flowers are small and inconspicuous, occurring in loose spikes. Heart-shaped leaves with pointed tips. Habitat: arable fields. Common throughout in suitable habitat.

Confusion plant: none.

Pink Purslane
Claytonia sibirica
Height: Up to 40 cm
Flower: 1–1.4 cm, Apr–Oct
A short, hairless plant with slightly fleshy leaves. Flowers are pink with five deeply notched petals. Leaves are oval and unstalked, occurring in opposite pairs. Habitat: damp woodlands and riversides. A naturalized species spreading particularly along rivers and streams.

Confusion plant: none.

Broad-leaved Dock

Rumex obtusifolius
Height: 50–150 cm
Flower: 0.1–0.3 cm, May–Oct
An erect plant with stout, much-branched stem. The tiny flowers are reddish or green, and are carried in whorls on leafy spikes. Broad, oblong dark green leaves have hairs on the veins beneath. Habitat: waste ground, grassland, arable fields, hedgerows. Common throughout in suitable habitat.

Confusion plants: there are several species of dock for which a specialist book will be required.

Spear-leaved Orache

Atriplex prostrata
Height: 30–100 cm
Flower: Tiny, Jul–Oct
Erect or prostrate; white, sometimes red-striped stems; unattractive. Tiny, unisexual flowers in clusters. Leaves spear-shaped; green, slightly mealy in texture underneath. Habitat: waste ground, especially near the coast. Common throughout in suitable habitat.

Confusion plants: Common Orache, *Atriplex patula*, has narrow, pointed leaves, lowest lobe usually pointing slightly forwards; Good King Henry, *Chenopodium bonus-henricus*, has flowers in a leafless spike, leaves almost untoothed, and often reddish stems.

Sea Beet (Wild Beet)

Beta vulgaris subsp. *maritima*
Height: 30–80 cm
Flower: 0.3–0.4 cm, Jun–Sep
Sprawling and untidy-looking plant of seaside; fleshy and often reddish. Flowers green and tiny, in clusters which occur in spikes. Leaves triangular, oval or heart-shaped; tough and shiny green with long stems. Grows on wasteground by the sea, saltmarshes, beaches and among coastal rocks. Common throughout in suitable habitat.

Confusion plant: none.

Glasswort
(Marsh Samphire)
Salicornia europaea
Height: 5–25 cm
Flower: 0.1 cm, Jul–Sep
Small, erect, fleshy plant with cylindrical stems which vary in colour from yellowish green to red. The tiny flowers, which occur at the stem joints, are insignificant. Leaves are essentially just extensions of the stems in colour and form. Grows on saltmarshes. Uncommon due to a lack of saltmarsh across most of the county.

Confusion plant: none.

Spring Sandwort
Minuartia verna
Height: 5–20 cm
Flower: 0.7–0.9 cm, May–Sep
Low, patch-forming plant with downy stems, easily overlooked. White flowers have five petals, slightly longer than the green sepals between them. Narrow, almost moss-like leaves occur in tufts around the stem. Habitat: short grassland near the coast on rocks. Uncommon, the Lizard peninsula around Kynance is good.

Confusion plants: Fine-leaved Sandwort, *Minuartia hybrida*; Thyme-leaved Sandwort, *Arenaria serpyllifolia*, and Mossy Sandwort, *Arenaria balearica*, are also found in Cornwall; a specialist guide will identify these.

Common Mouse-ear
Cerastium fontanum
Height: 20–45 cm
Flower: 0.8–1.2 cm, Apr–Nov
Low-growing, usually with hairy stems. White flowers have five notched petals; petals and sepals approximately the same length. Leaves narrow and oval. Habitat: waste ground, arable fields and grassland. Common throughout in suitable habitat.

Confusion plants: Several other Mouse-ears occur in Cornwall, including Sticky Mouse-ear, *Cerastium glomeratum*, which has stickily hairy leaves.

Greater Stitchwort
Stellaria holostea
Height: 20–70 cm
Heads: 1.5–2.5 cm, Mar–Jun
A slender, rough-edged, trailing plant, which often forms patches. The white flowers have five petals which are deeply divided, almost appearing as ten petals, each petal is veined; the yellow stamens are usually obvious. Leaves are narrow and pointed. Habitat: woodland, hedgerows and roadsides.

Common throughout in suitable habitat.

Confusion plant: Lesser Stitchwort, *Stellaria graminea*, has smaller flowers (0.5–1.2 cm), in which the petals only just match the sepals in length; it also has smooth stems; flowering time: May–Sep.

The greater stitchwort is a very distinctive flower of Cornish hedgerows in spring. As such it has developed a fair amount of local folklore. The plant was originally named because it was used to cure a stitch in the stomach.

Some people believed that pixies hid among the greater stitchwort's foliage, others that it was adders that could be found there, so to pick its flowers would risk upsetting the pixies or being bitten by an adder.

Rock Sea Spurrey
Spergularia rupicola
Height: 10–40 cm
Heads: 0.8–1 cm, Jun–Sep
Low-growing, with hairs, often forming patches. Flowers pink, usually whiter in the centre; the five petals equal in length to the five sepals. Leaves narrow, but slightly fleshy, occurring in opposite pairs. Usually grows on rocky ground by the sea. Uncommon.

Confusion plants: Greater Sea Spurrey, *Spergularia media*, is hairless and has petals longer than sepals; petals a bluer pink; on saltmarshes and beaches; Lesser Sea Spurrey, *Spergularia marina*, has smaller flowers (0.5–0.8 cm) and petals shorter than sepals; usually on saltmarshes.

Sea Campion
Silene uniflora
Height: 15–30 cm
Heads: 2–2.5 cm, Apr–Sep
A patch-forming plant with slightly downy stems. The white flowers have five notched petals and a deep, bladder-like calyx tube, which is reddish in colour, behind the petals. Leaves are greyish-green, spear-shaped and occur in opposite pairs. Habitat: coastal, on beaches, maritime grassland and on rocks. Common throughout in suitable habitat.

Confusion plant: Bladder Campion, *Silene vulgaris*, has branched stems, more upright and smaller flowers.

Ragged Robin
Lychnis flos-cuculi
Height: 25–80 cm
Heads: 2–3 cm, May–Aug
An erect plant with dark reddish stems. Pink flowers with five deeply cut, long, thin petals giving the impression of a tatty red campion. Leaves narrow and spear-shaped, occurring in opposite pairs. Grows in damp meadows, marshes and wet woodlands. Common throughout in suitable habitat.

Confusion plant: none.

Red Campion
Silene dioica
Height: 20–80 cm
Flower: 1.5–2.5 cm, Mar–Nov
An erect, hairy plant with dark stems. Flowers are pink; the five petals are deeply notched; flower has a dark, veined calyx tube. The leaves are spear-shaped and hairy. Habitat: woodland, hedges and various others. Common throughout in suitable habitat.

Confusion plant: none.

White Campion
Silene latifolia
Height: 30–100 cm
Flower: 2–3 cm, May–Oct
An erect, softly hairy plant with branched stems. Flowers white, the five petals deeply notched; has a softly hairy calyx tube. Leaves are spear-shaped, occurring in opposite pairs. Habitat: arable fields, hedges and roadsides. Widespread, but not common.

Confusion plant: Night-flowering Catchfly, *Silene noctiflora*, is stickily hairy with a pinkish wash to the petals, which open at night; shorter than white campion; quite rare, occurring in arable fields (West Pentire).

Small-flowered Catchfly
Silene gallica
Height: 10–45 cm
Flower: 1–1.2 cm, Jun–Oct
Small, erect plant with downy stem. Flowers small and white with five notched petals; often all the flowers on a stem point in the same direction. Leaves are spear-shaped and stickily hairy. Habitat: arable fields and sandy places. Rare, West Pentire is a good location.

Confusion plant: Night-flowering Catchfly, *Silene noctiflora*, is stickily hairy with a pinkish wash to the petals which open at night; flowers larger than small-flowered catchfly; quite rare, occurring in arable fields (West Pentire).

White Water-lily

Nymphaea alba
Height: 100–300 cm
Flower: 9–20 cm, Jun–Sep
Aquatic plant whose stems are submerged and whose leaves and flowers float on the surface. The cup-shaped flowers are fragrant and white. Leaves are almost circular, tough and dark green. Grows in ponds and lakes. Common throughout in suitable habitat.

Confusion plants: Yellow Water-lily, *Nuphar lutea*, has much smaller, less elaborate, yellow flowers, and escaped garden water lilies have a variety of colours.

Love-in-a-mist

Nigelle damascena
Height: 10–30 cm
Flower: 2–3 cm, Jun–Sep
Slender, erect, much-branched plant. The flower has five blue sepals surrounded by feathery, thin leaves which are greatly divided. Habitat: waste ground, arable fields and gardens. Common in gardens.

Confusion plant: none.

Marsh marigold (Kingcup)

Caltha palustris
Height: 10–50 cm
Flower: 2–5 cm, Mar–Jul
Clump-forming, hairless plant. Large, yellow, buttercup-type flowers. Heart-shaped, dark green leaves grow up to 10 cm across. Habitat: marshes, damp grassland, ditches and damp woodland. Common throughout in suitable habitat.

Confusion plant: none.

Meadow Buttercup

Ranunculus acris
Height: 30–100 cm
Flower: 1.5–2.5 cm, Apr–Oct
Erect, hairy plant. The flowers have five petals and are yellow and shiny. The leaves are deeply divided. Habitat: grassland, woodland clearings, roadside verges and hedges. This is the commonest of the buttercup varieties.

Confusion plants: other buttercup species can be confused, one key to identification is in the shape of the leaf, since other species have leaves which are not so deeply divided.

Lesser Celandine

Ranunculus ficaria
Height: 5–25 cm
Flower: 1.5–3 cm, Feb–May
A low-growing, patch-forming, hairless plant. The shiny yellow flowers have 8 to 12 narrow petals. The leaves are heart-shaped and dark green, sometimes blotched darker. Habitat: woodlands, hedges and riverbanks. Common throughout in suitable habitat.

Confusion plant: none.

Traveller's Joy (Old Man's Beard)

Clematis vitalba
Height: Up to 10 m
Flower: 1–2 cm, Jul–Sep
A woody, climbing clematis which scrambles untidily over trees and walls; distinctive in autumn and winter when fluffy seedheads form (resembling an 'old man's beard'); photo shows an example just starting to go to seed. Creamy white flowers with four sepals, rather than petals, and numerous stamens. Leaves are compound with five leaflets in opposite pairs. Habitat: roadsides, railway embankments, hedges and woodland. Common throughout in suitable habitat.

Confusion plant: none.

Columbine
Aquilegia vulgaris
Height: 30–100 cm
Flower: 3–5 cm, May–Jul
Erect plant with much-branched, downy stem. The violet-blue, intricate flowers grow at the top of nodding stems. The compound leaves, which grow from near the base of the plant, are split into three heart-shaped, lobed leaflets. Habitat: woods and scrub; also a garden escape. Infrequent.

Confusion plant: none.

Wood Anemone
Anemone nemorosa
Height: 8–25 cm
Flower: 2–4 cm, Mar–May
Clump-forming plant covering the ground but not growing very tall. White, sometimes pinkish flowers; formed by sepals rather than petals which usually number between six and nine; occur at the top of flimsy stems, often nodding and half closing in dull conditions. Leaves much divided and hairless. Habitat: woodland and hedges. Common throughout in suitable habitat.

Confusion plant: none.

Common Fumitory
Fumaria officinalis
Height: 10–40 cm
Flower: 0.7–1 cm, Apr–Oct
A scrambling plant. Flowers are pink with darker tips, occurring in spikes of at least 20 flowers. Leaves are fine, almost fern-like. Habitat: waste ground and arable fields. Common throughout in suitable habitat.

Confusion plants: Common Ramping Fumitory, *Fumaria muralis*; Tall Ramping Fumitory, *Fumaria bastardii*; White Ramping Fumitory, *Fumaria capreolata* and Purple Ramping Fumitory, *Fumaria purpurea* all occur, and a specialist guide is necessary to separate these species.

Common Poppy

Papaver rhoeas
Height: 20–80 cm
Flower: 5–10 cm, May–Sep
An erect plant (top left) with bristly stems. Scarlet-red flowers with four overlapping silky petals and a dark centre. Roughly hairy, compound leaves, deeply cut and toothed. Habitat: arable fields. Widespread, growing in great abundance where found.

Confusion plants: Rough Poppy, *Papaver hybridum* (left), is smaller with crimson-red petals which do not overlap; Long-headed Poppy, *Papaver dubium* (top right), has orange-red petals without dark centres, and a long seed pod; both of these are very rare and occur at West Pentire.

The name of the commonest arable weed, the common poppy, probably derives from the plant's Latin name *papaver*, but its close association with humans has led to the formation of many infrequently used local names, such as 'Thunderflower', 'Blind Eyes' and 'Wart Flower', because it was said that those picking its flowers were likely to be struck by lightning, become blind or grow warts. It is thought such names developed to discourage children from picking them, and damaging the crops in which they grew.

Yellow Horned Poppy (Horned Poppy)
Glaucium flavum
Height: 30–100 cm
Flower: 5–10 cm, Jun–Sep
A large, sprawling plant with greyish-green leaves and long, horn-shaped seed pods. The flamboyant yellow petals are flimsy. The leaves are wavy-edged and deeply lobed. Habitat: shingle beaches and dunes. Uncommon.

Confusion plant: none.

Charlock
Sinapis arvensis
Height: 20–130 cm
Flower: 1–1.7 cm, Mar–Jul
An erect and branched, roughly hairy plant. The yellow flowers have four petals which are arranged in a cross; the flowers are borne in domed clusters. The leaves are toothed and irregularly lobed; they are larger lower down and narrower higher up the plant. Habitat: arable fields, hedges and roadsides. Can be extremely numerous as an arable weed.

Confusion plant: White Mustard, *Sinapis alba*, is less common and has deeply lobed leaves.

Black Mustard
Brassica nigra
Height: 40–150 cm
Flower: 0.8–1 cm, Apr–Sep
Tall, much-branched member of the cabbage family; slender stems but quite strong. Yellow flowers have four petals arranged in a cross, in clusters which increase in length as the lower fruits mature (fruits up to 2 cm long). Lower leaves are hairy; leaves are split into large lobes, of which the end lobe is the largest. Habitat: roadside verges, cliff tops and waste ground. Very common.

Confusion plants: Hoary Mustard, *Hirschfeldia incana*, is less common; has paler flowers and coarse hairs; Charlock, *Sinapis arvensis*, in arable fields, has much longer fruits than black mustard (2.5–4.5 cm).

Garlic Mustard
Alliaria petiolata
Height: 50–120 cm
Flower: 0.5–0.8 cm, Apr–Jul
An erect, hairless plant with large leaves topped by small clusters of flowers, smells of garlic when crushed. Flower is white with four petals occurring in clusters at the top of the stems. Large, heart-shaped leaves with toothed edges, often slightly bronzed in colour. Habitat: hedges and open woodland. Common throughout in suitable habitat.

Confusion plant: none.

Cuckoo Flower (Lady's Smock)
Cardamine pratensis
Height: 30–55 cm
Flower: 0.8–1.3 cm, Apr–Jul
An erect, thin-stemmed plant. Flowers have four pink or lilac petals, each with a notch; these are carried in clusters at the tops of the stems. Leaves at base are compound with oval leaflets; those on the stems are smaller and narrower. Habitat: wet grassland and freshwater marshes. Common throughout in suitable habitat

Confusion plant: none.

Sea Rocket
Cakile maritima
Height: 15–50 cm
Flower: 0.6–1.2 cm, Apr–Sep
A sprawling plant which rises towards the flowerheads; greyish-green and fleshy. Flowers usually white or pale pink, but can be violet; four small petals form a cross; flowers occur in clusters at the stem tips. Leaves are fleshy and narrowly spoon-shaped with toothed edges. Found growing at the seaward edge of sand dunes and the uppermost parts of beaches. Widespread.

Confusion plant: none.

Common Scurvy-grass
Cochlearia officinalis
Height: 10–50 cm
Flower: 0.6–1 cm, Mar–May
A fleshy, sprawling plant with glossy appearance. Flowers have four white petals in a cross, and occur in clusters; at first half hidden by foliage, the clusters elongate into spikes as the plant matures. Dark green and kidney-shaped leaves; fleshy; only lower leaves are stalked. Saltmarshes, coastal grasslands, hedges. Common throughout in suitable habitat.

Confusion plant: Early Scurvy-grass, *Cochlearia danica*, often has lilac flowers; can flower earlier in year; has stalked upper leaves.

Shepherd's Purse
Capsella bursa-pastoris
Height: 5–50 cm
Flower: 0.2–0.4 cm, Feb–Nov
An erect plant with characteristically shaped seed pods, likened to a shepherd's purse. Tiny and white with four petals, occurring in flat-topped spikes which continue to grow as the seed pods develop. Spear-shaped leaves along stem, while at base the leaves are oval and toothed. Habitat: gardens and arable fields. Common throughout in suitable habitat.

Confusion plant: none.

Opposite-leaved Saxifrage
Chrysosplenium oppositifolium
Height: 5–20 cm
Flower: 0.4–0.6 cm, Mar–Jul
Low growing, creeping plant, with leafy stems and inconspicuous flowers. Flowers are yellow and occur in a flat leafy cluster at the tips of the stems. Leaves occur in opposite pairs around the stem, and are almost circular but slightly toothed. Habitat: woodlands, particularly where wet. Common throughout in suitable habitat.

Confusion plant: none.

Oblong-leaved Sundew
Drosera intermedia
Height: 2–5 cm
Flower: 0.2–0.4 cm, Jun–Aug
A tiny insectivorous plant with a reddish colour. Small flowers are white and have five petals; they are borne on long stems. Oval-shaped leaves are covered in sticky 'dew' on 'hairs'; they occur as a basal rosette. Habitat: peat bogs; Bodmin Moor and Goss Moor are good. Uncommon.

Confusion plant: Round-leaved Sundew, *Drosera intermedia*, is also present in Cornwall, and can be distinguished because of its round leaves.

Wild Mignonette
Reseda lutea
Height: 20–80 cm
Flower: 0.4–0.8 cm, Jun–Sep
An erect, leafy plant growing in clumps. The small, pale yellow flowers are borne in tall flower spikes; each flower has six sepals and petals. The leaves have wavy margins, and are cut into three to five pointed lobes. Habitat: mostly sand dunes. Common throughout in suitable habitat.

Confusion plant: Weld, *Reseda luteola*, is similar, but each flower has four sepals and petals.

Navelwort (Pennywort)
Umbilicus rupestris
Height: 10–80 cm
Flower: 0.5–1 cm, May–Aug
An erect, fleshy plant growing from walls. The small, greenish-yellow (fading to brown) flowers are tubular in shape and are borne in tall flower spikes. The leaves are fleshy and approximately circular, with a central depression (hence 'navel'). Habitat: hedges and walls. Common throughout in suitable habitat.

Confusion plant: none.

Biting Stonecrop
Sedum acre
Height: 5–10 cm
Flower: 1–1.2 cm, May–Aug
A fleshy plant which forms cushion-shaped patches close to the ground. The yellow flowers have five narrow petals which face upwards. Tiny, scale-like fleshy leaves along stem. Habitat: sand dunes and rocky places. Common throughout in suitable habitat.

Confusion plant: none.

English Stonecrop
Sedum anglicum
Height: 5–10 cm
Flower: 1–1.2 cm, Jun–Sep
A fleshy, mat-forming plant. Flowers are white above and pinkish below, each facing upwards from the tops of stems. Leaves are small and fleshy. Grows among stones and rocks, particularly on coast and waste ground. Common throughout in suitable habitat.

Confusion plant: none.

Agrimony
Agrimonia eupatoria
Height: 20–120 cm
Flower: 0.5–0.8 cm, Jun–Aug
Softly hairy plant which grows a tall flower spike, often in clusters; where it grows on the coast it rarely reaches its full potential height. The small yellow flowers have five petals and occur in a tall, thin flower spike. Downy leaves are split into alternating large and small pairs of leaflets. Habitat: grassland and hedgerow, especially around the coast. Common throughout in suitable habitat.

Confusion plant: Fragrant Agrimony, *Agrimonia procera*, also found in Cornwall and Scilly; it is fragrant and hairier.

Meadowsweet
Filipendula ulmaria
Height: 50–120 cm
Flower: 0.3–0.8 cm, Jun–Oct
An erect plant with long leafy stems; hairless. Creamy white, small flowers occur in 'frothy' heads; very sweet scented. Compound leaves, each leaflet is oval and toothed with hairs underneath. Habitat: marshy ground, often beside streams. Common throughout in suitable habitat.

Confusion plant: none.

Great Burnet
Sanguisorba officinalis
Height: 10–90 cm
Heads: 1–2 cm, Jun–Sep
An erect plant with tall, thin-branched stems. The wine-red flowers are packed into dense, oblong heads. The leaf is divided into three to seven leaflets, each of which is toothed, and the largest one is at the tip of the leaf. Habitat: damp meadows. Uncommon, a good location is at Goonhilly Downs.

Confusion plant: none.

Dog Rose
Rosa canina
Height: 100–300 cm
Flower: 2–6 cm, May–Jul
A scrambling, shrubby plant with arching stem and sharp, curving thorns; red hips in late summer. The pale pink flowers have five petals, and the numerous stamens are obvious. The leaves are divided into three to five oval-shaped leaflets, each with a toothed edge. Habitat: hedges, scrub, woodland edges. Common throughout in suitable habitat.

Confusion plants: Field Rose, *Rosa arvensis*, always has white petals; the garden escape, *Rosa rugosa*, has much more flamboyant, deep pink flowers and larger hips.

Burnet Rose

Rosa pimpinellifolia
Height: 20–100 cm
Flower: 2–4 cm, May–Jul

A scrambling, shrubby plant with straight thorns; hips are purplish-red. The flowers have five petals and are creamy-yellow. The leaves are divided into three to five small rounded, but toothed, leaflets. Habitat: hedges, rocky areas and dunes. Uncommon but widespread.

Confusion plant: Field Rose, *Rosa arvensis*, has white flowers and curved thorns.

Bramble

Rubus fruticosus
Height: 100–400 cm
Flower: 2–3 cm, May–Nov

A scrambling plant with fierce thorns. The flowers have five petals and are pink, white or purplish with numerous stamens. Leaves have three to five leaflets, each of which has a prickly vein. Habitat: hedgerows, waste ground and woodland. Common throughout in suitable habitat.

Confusion plant: none.

Wood Avens (Herb Bennet)

Geum urbanum
Height: 20–50 cm
Flower: 1–1.5 cm, May–Sep

An erect plant with downy stem; has distinctive fruits with a cluster of hooks which attach to clothing. Flowers are yellow with five petals, and five narrow sepals visible between the petals. Leaves are split into three or five leaflets, in which the end leaflet is the biggest. Habitat: hedgerows, woodland and shady places. Common throughout in suitable habitat.

Confusion plant: none.

Marsh Cinquefoil
Potentilla palustris
Height: 20–60 cm
Flower: 2–3 cm, May–Jul
An erect plant with tall, thin but robust stems. The flowers are reddish-purple with five small, narrow petals and five much larger sepals which form a star shape. Leaves are split into three to seven leaflets; each is toothed, and the last one is the largest. Habitat: marshes and ditches. Uncommon, the wet moors in central Cornwall (Goss, Breney etc.) are good for this species.

Confusion plant: none.

Wild Strawberry
Fragaria vesca
Height: 5–15 cm
Flower: 1.2–1.8 cm, Apr–Jul
Sprawling plant with runners and hairy stems; has small strawberries later in year. White flowers have five white, almost circular petals. Three coarsely toothed leaflets make up each leaf; these are silkily hairy beneath and yellowish green in colour. Habitat: hedges and woodland edges. Common throughout in suitable habitat.

Confusion plant: Barren Strawberry, *Potentilla sterilis*, has greyish-green, coarsely hairy leaves; its flowers have notched petals with large gaps between; has no strawberries.

Silverweed
Potentilla anserina
Height: 10–30 cm
Flower: 1.5–2 cm, May–Sep
Prostrate plant with numerous red runners, and an overall silvery-hairy texture. The yellow flowers have five petals. Leaves are split into between three and 12 pairs of leaflets, which are all toothed and silvery underneath. Habitat: damp grassland, pebbly ground, at the back of beaches and on waste ground. Common throughout in suitable habitat.

Confusion plant: none.

Tormentil
Potentilla erecta
Height: 10–40 cm
Flower: 0.8–1.6 cm, May–Oct
Creeping, prostrate plant with downy stems. The small, yellow flowers have four notched petals and obvious sepals. The leaves along the stems are deeply cut, almost forming five pointed leaflets. Habitat: grassland, moorland and coastal heath. Common throughout in suitable habitat.

Confusion plants: several potentilla species only distinguished with a specialist guide.

Broom
Cytisus scoparius
Height: 100–250 cm
Flower: 1.5–2.5 cm, Apr–Jul
A much branched, twiggy-looking bush; has long black seed pods. Yellow flowers growing along the sides of the stems towards their tops, often having the effect of smothering the bush. Small, unobtrusive leaves, sometimes split into three leaflets. Habitat: varied including hedges, waste ground, railway embankments. Widespread, but never as common as gorse.

Confusion plant: Gorse, *Ulex europaeus*, has a similar superficial appearance, but has spines which the broom does not.

Dyer's Greenweed
Genista tinctoria
Height: 10–100 cm
Flower: 1.2–1.8 cm, Jun–Aug
A creeping plant with erect flower stems. Yellow flowers are carried in blunt, spike-shaped heads. Leaves are narrow and oval, slightly hairy. Habitat: grassland, mostly coastal. Widespread on coast.

Confusion plant: Hairy Greenweed, *Genista pilosa*, is far less common, and has densely hairy leaves.

Gorse (Furze)

Ulex europaeus
Height: 100–300 cm
Flower: 1.5–2 cm, Oct–Jul

A dense, dark, woody, spiny shrub; distinctive seed pods which pop as they split. The yellow flowers have a coconut scent and are borne in spikes. The leaves are essentially just spines. Habitat: waste ground, coast, roadsides, heaths and moors. Common throughout in suitable habitat.

Confusion plant: Western Gorse, *Ulex gallii* (right), is shorter and less bushy, often grows low down with heather; it has deeper yellow flowers from July to September, mostly coastal distribution.

'Kissing is in season when gorse is in blossom', or words to that effect, indicate a long flowering season for gorse. This season is made even longer by the fact that we have two species which flower at different times of year. Gorse is an important shrub around our coastline for nesting birds such as the stonechat, linnet and whitethroat; it is also the food plant of the green hairstreak butterfly's caterpillar, making this a good plant on which to locate this species.

Tufted Vetch
Vicia cracca
Height: 50–200 cm
Flower: 0.8–1.5 cm, Jun–Sep
A scrambling plant with long twisting tendrils. The flowers are bluish-purple with between 10 and 40 small flowers in each one-sided head. The leaves are divided into eight to 12 narrow leaflets. Habitat: hedgerows and scrub land. Common throughout in suitable habitat.

Confusion plant: Fodder Vetch, *Vicia villosa*, has leaves split into six to eight leaflets, and often has yellow or white wings to flowers.

Hairy Tare
Vicia hirsuta
Height: 20–70 cm
Flower: 0.2–0.4 cm, May–Aug
A thin, hairy, much-branched, scrambling plant. The tiny, pale lilac flowers occur in spikes of between one and six. The leaves are divided into four to ten tiny, thin leaflets. Habitat: grassland, hedges, arable fields and waste ground. Common throughout in suitable habitat.

Confusion plant: Smooth Tare, *Vicia tetrasperma*, has three to six leaflets, deep lilac flowers, and hairless seed pods.

Common Vetch
Vicia sativa
Height: 20–100 cm
Flower: 1–2 cm, Apr–Sep
A trailing, climbing plant often forming patches. The flowers are deep reddish-purple, occurring in pairs or singly. The leaves are divided into three to six pairs of leaflets, each oval in shape. Habitat: grassland, hedges and waste ground. Common throughout in suitable habitat.

Confusion plant: none.

Kidney Vetch
Anthyllis vulneraria
Height: 10–60 cm
Flower: 1.2–1.5 cm, Apr–Sep
Prostrate, sprawling and silkily hairy. Yellow flowers are shaped typically of the pea family, but they occur in densely packed, paired heads, one half of each head maturing before the other. Leaves are compound with small, narrowly oval leaflets. Grows mostly on rocky coastlines. Common throughout in suitable habitat.

Confusion plant: none.

Restharrow
Ononis repens
Height: 10–60 cm
Flower: 1.5–2 cm, Jun–Sep
A prostrate/semi-erect plant with stickily hairy covering, can become quite dense and difficult to move, hence name. Pink flowers with white centres are borne in loose spikes. Leaves split into three narrow, oval leaflets. Habitat: grassland, often dunes. Common throughout in suitable habitat.

Confusion plant: none.

Black Medick
Medicago lupulina
Height: 10–50 cm
Heads: 0.3–1 cm, Apr–Oct
Prostrate or semi-erect plant, usually downy; seed pods are black. Between 10 and 50 tiny yellow flowers are borne in spherical heads. Leaves are trifoliate, clover-like. Habitat: grassland, hedges and roadsides. Very common.

Confusion plants: Lesser Trefoil, *Trifolium dubium*, is similar but hairless, and has brown seed pods; Spotted Medick, *Medicago arabica*, has dark spot on leaves, and only between one and four flowers in each head.

Bird's Foot Trefoil (Eggs and Bacon)

Lotus corniculatus
Height: 5–60 cm
Flower: 1–1.8 cm, May–Oct

A prostrate plant often with downy stem; seed pods are straight and resemble a bird's foot. Yellow or sometimes orange flowers are pea-like. Leaves are comprised of five small leaflets, two of which hug the stem. Habitat: meadows and coastal areas. Very common.

Confusion plant: several similar species occur in Cornwall; a specialist guide will be necessary to identify them.

The bird's foot trefoil is a very common plant around the coast of Cornwall. The term 'trefoil' is a bit misleading, since this species has five leaflets, but because two of them hug the stem it looks like three leaflets. One insect that depends upon it is the six-spot burnet moth, a black and red day-flying moth; the caterpillars of this moth (right) eat the leaves of this trefoil.

White Clover

Trifolium repens
Height: 20–50 cm
Heads: 1–3 cm, May–Nov
Prostrate with erect, leafless flower stems. White, spherical flower heads are borne on long flower stems. Leaves are trifoliate with a whitish mark. Habitat: grassland of all types. Very common; the Lizard peninsula around Caerthillian Cove is renowned for its huge variety of clovers, the identification of which requires a specialist field guide.

Confusion plant: Red Clover, *Trifolium pratense*, is similar but with reddish-purple flowers.

Common Storksbill

Erodium cicutarium
Height: 5–60 cm
Flower: 1–2 cm, Apr–Oct
A sprawling plant; hairy, sometimes a little sticky. Purple, pink or white flowers with five petals. Fern-like and hairy leaves. Habitat: sand dunes. Common throughout in suitable habitat

Confusion plant: none.

Wood Sorrel

Oxalis acetosella
Height: 10–20 cm
Flower: 0.7–1.4 cm, Mar–May
A delicate plant forming small clumps. The bell-shaped white, nodding flowers have pinkish veins. The leaves are trifoliate, the three leaflets gathering in a pyramidal shape. Habitat: woodland, hedges and even on trees among moss. Common throughout in suitable habitat

Confusion plant: none.

Cut-leaved Cranesbill

Geranium dissectum
Height: 10–50 cm
Flower: 0.5–1 cm, May–Oct
Semi-erect with hairy stem; fruits are shaped like cranes' bills. Flowers are pink with five notched petals. Leaves are deeply divided into narrow segments. Habitat: grassland and hedges. Common throughout in suitable habitat.

Confusion plant: many other cranesbills are present, including the Meadow Cranesbill, *Geranium pratense*, which has bluer, larger flowers, and slightly less deeply cut leaves; and Hedgerow Cranesbill, *Geranium pyrenaicum*, which has less deeply cut leaves.

Hedgerow Cranesbill

Geranium pyrenaicum
Height: 10–70 cm
Flower: 1.2–1.8 cm, May–Sep
Semi-erect plant. The flowers are pink with five notched petals. The leaves are cut about half way, and are only sparsely hairy. Habitat: grassland and hedgerow. Common throughout in suitable habitat.

Confusion plant: Cut-leaved Cranesbill, *Geranium dissectum*, has more deeply cut leaves.

Herb Robert

Geranium robertianum
Height: 20–50 cm
Flower: 1.5–3 cm, May–Nov
An erect, strong-smelling plant with hairy stems often tinged with red. Pink flowers have five petals and orange stamens. The leaves are fern-like and hairy. Habitat: hedgerows, woodland and anywhere with shade. Common throughout in suitable habitat.

Confusion plant: none.

Bloody Cranesbill

Geranium sanguineum
Height: 20–100 cm
Flower: 2–3 cm, May–Aug
A semi-erect plant with woody base and dense foliage. The reddish-purple flowers have five notched petals. The leaves are dark green, deeply cut and hairy. Habitat: coastal on rocky ground. Rare, Kynance Cove is a good location.

Confusion plant: none.

Sun Spurge

Euphorbia helioscopia
Height: 10–50 cm
Flower: 0.1–0.2 cm, Apr–Nov
An erect plant, yellowish-green and hairless, can have a reddish stem; has white sap in stem. Tiny flower without sepals or petals, being carried in flat-topped clusters. Leaves are circular and finely toothed, pale green and hairless. Habitat: waste ground and arable fields. Common throughout in suitable habitat.

Confusion plant: all spurges have many similar features, but this species should be identifiable by a mixture of the listed attributes.

Sea Spurge

Euphorbia paralias
Height: 10–70 cm
Flower: 0.1–0.2 cm, Jun–Sep
An erect plant branched only at the base; grey-green in colour; has white sap in stem. Tiny flower without sepals or petals, being carried at the tops of the stems. Leaves are oval and fleshy, occurring densely around the stem. Habitat: sand dunes and beaches. Common throughout in suitable habitat.

Confusion plant: the leafy stem and habitat should be enough to identify this species from other spurges.

Dog's Mercury
Mercurialis perennis
Height: 20–40 cm
Flower: 0.4–0.5 cm, Jan–May
Erect plant forming extensive patches in undisturbed woodland. Small green flowers are carried in thin spikes, males and females occurring on different plants. Leaves oval and pointed with toothed margin, occurring in opposite pairs. Habitat: woodland and shady hedges. Common throughout in suitable habitat.

Confusion plant: none.

Milkwort
Polygala vulgaris
Height: 5–30 cm
Flower: 0.4–0.7 cm, Apr–Sep
A sprawling, prostrate plant which grows half hidden among other vegetation. The small flowers are usually blue or purplish-blue, but sometimes white or pink; they are carried in clusters. The leaves are oval but narrow. Habitat: moor, heath, and particularly coastal. Common throughout in suitable habitat.

Confusion plant: none.

Musk Mallow
Malva moschata
Height: 20–90 cm
Flower: 2.5–5 cm, Jul–Oct
An erect plant with hairy stems. Flowers are rose-pink with five flimsy petals which are almost square-cut; flowers are borne in very loose spikes. Leaves are deeply and narrowly cut. Habitat: hedgerows, grassland and roadside verges. Common throughout in suitable habitat.

Confusion plant: similar to other mallows (such as Rough Mallow, *Althaea hirsuta*), but combination of flower colour and leaf shape are enough to identify this species.

Common Mallow
Malva sylvestris
Height: 20–100 cm
Flower: 2–4 cm, Jun–Nov
A sprawling plant with substantial stems and downy texture. Flowers are pink with purple veining; the five thin petals are notched. Leaves often kidney-shaped and irregularly fringed with a dark spot. Habitat: hedgerows, roadsides, grassland and coastal. Common throughout in suitable habitat.

Confusion plant: Tree Mallow, *Lavatera arborea*, is taller (up to 3 m), with a woody base to the stem; it also has darker purple flowers.

Slender St John's Wort
Hypericum pulchrum
Height: 20–80 cm
Flower: 1.2–1.8 cm, Jul–Sep
An erect plant with stiff, hairless stems. Flowers are yellow and have five petals; often red-tinged beneath and when in bud. Leaves oval and occurring in opposite pairs from the stem. Habitat: grassland, heathland and woods. Common throughout in suitable habitat.

Confusion plants: many other types of St John's Wort occur in Cornwall; a specialist guide will be necessary to identify them.

Sweet Violet
Viola odorata
Height: 5–15 cm
Flower: 0.8–1.5 cm, Feb–May
A short plant with creeping nature and plenty of leaves; the flowers are scented. The flowers are usually violet in colour, though can be white, pink or even yellow. The leaves are heart-shaped though quite circular, dark green with a scalloped edge. Habitat: woodland margins and hedges. Fairly common.

Confusion plant: the Hairy Violet, *Viola hirta*, has longer leaves and more hairs, with unscented flowers.

Common Dog Violet

Viola riviniana
Height: 5–10 cm
Flower: 1.5–2.5 cm, Feb–Jun
A low, tufted plant with runners. The flowers are violet in colour with a cream-coloured spur (the long, narrow extension to the flower behind the petals). The leaves are heart-shaped and slightly scalloped. Habitat: woodland, hedges, scrub and grassland. Common throughout in suitable habitat.

Confusion plant: Early Dog Violet, *Viola reichenbachiana*, has a violet spur behind the petals, and narrower leaves.

The common dog violet is an important species because its leaves are eaten by the caterpillars of several fritillary butterflies, including the pearl-bordered, small pearl-bordered (right) and dark green fritillaries. This species grows well in coppiced woodland where sunlight can reach the ground in areas where trees have just been cut down.

Butterwort
Pinguicula vulgaris
Height: 5–10 cm
Flower: 1–1.5 cm, May–Jul
An erect flower stem with basal rosette of leaves. Purple flowers, with spurs, are borne at the top of slender nodding stems. The leaves are oval and have curled edges which trap insects. Habitat: bogs, marshes and wet heaths. Common throughout in suitable habitat.

Confusion plant: the Pale Butterwort, *Pinguicula lusitanica*, has pale lilac flowers and a down-turned spur.

Wild Pansy
Viola tricolor
Height: 5–25 cm
Flower: 1.5–2.5 cm, Apr–Nov
A semi-erect plant with fairly weak stems. The flowers are violet or yellow and violet; the petals longer than the sepals. The leaves are stalked, oval and toothed. Habitat: grassland, dunes and heaths. Uncommon.

Confusion plant: the Field Pansy, *Viola arvensis*, is found on arable land and has much smaller, creamy-yellow flowers in which the sepals are longer than the petals.

Enchanter's Nightshade
Circaea lutetiana
Height: 10–40 cm
Flower: 0.5–0.7 cm, Jun–Sep
An erect, slightly hairy plant. White or sometimes pink flowers with four petals and long stamens; they are carried in loose flower spikes which become longer as the flower ages. The leaves are heart-shaped and quite dark green, occurring in opposite pairs. Habitat: woodland and shady hedges. Common throughout in suitable habitat.

Confusion plant: none.

Evening Primrose

Oenothera biennis
Height: 80–150 cm
Flower: 40–60 cm, Jun–Oct
A tall, erect, stout, downy plant. The large flowers are yellow and have four flimsy petals; they occur in tall spikes. The leaves are spear-shaped and downy. Habitat: waste ground, sand dunes and roadsides. Common throughout in suitable habitat.

Confusion plant: other Evening Primroses including the Large-flowered Evening Primrose, *Oenethera glazoviana*, has red hairs on stems, red-striped sepals and a white midrib on the leaves.

Rosebay Willowherb (Fireweed)

Chamerion angustifolium
Height: 80–250 cm
Flower: 2–3 cm, Jun–Sep
Erect, patch-forming, hairless plant. Flowers are reddish-pink, with four petals carried in spikes which become narrower at the top. The leaves are narrow and tapering. It is typically found along roadsides and railway lines, where its seed is carried by the wind; also found around woodland edges and on waste ground. Common throughout in suitable habitat.

Confusion plant: none.

Great Willowherb

Epilobium hirsutum
Height: 100–150 cm
Flower: 2–2.5 cm, Jun–Sep
Erect and downy, often forming patches. Flowers reddish-pink with four notched petals. Oval leaves occurring in pairs from stem. Habitat: marshes as well as dry ground, often found on waste land. Common throughout in suitable habitat.

Confusion plant: none.

Sea Holly

Eryngium maritimum
Height: 20–70 cm
Heads: 2–4 cm, Jul–Sep
Erect stems, but sprawling plant forming patches; bluish-green appearance. Many bluish-purple flowers cluster into spherical heads. Leaves shaped a little like a holly leaf, but more exaggerated, with longer and harder spines. Habitat: sand dunes and shingle beaches. Uncommon.
    Confusion plant: none.

The sea holly was so called because of its chosen habitat and its spiny leaves. Its bluish-green leaves are designed specifically to reduce water loss. Their unusual but rather attractive colour reflects the sun's heat better than simple green leaves, and they have a thick, waxy cuticle which helps to prevent water loss as well as protecting them against the effects of sea spray. In addition, the sea holly has incredibly deep roots for a plant of its size, sometimes getting as deep as two metres, and thus enabling it to find water which remains less tainted by salt. The sea holly has been used by people as food in various forms, including its shoots in salads and its roots as candied sweets, but its holly-like leaves have helped to prevent grazing by animals.

Purple Loosestrife
Lythrum salicaria
Height: 50–170 cm
Flower: 0.8–1.4 cm, Jun–Sep
An erect, hairy plant with stout stems and a patch-forming habit. Flowers are pinkish-purple and are borne in whorls around long, densely packed flower spikes. Leaves are spear-shaped and occur in whorls of three around the stem. Habitat: damp meadows, marshes and riversides. Common throughout in suitable habitat.

Confusion plant: none.

Ivy
Hedera helix
Height: 100–600 cm
Flower: 0.5–0.8 cm, Sep–Nov
A woody, climbing plant which grows along the ground or up trees and walls by means of small roots along its stem. Flowers yellowish-green and lacking petals. Leaves are glossy green and either have three lobes (on non-flowering shoots) or are oval. Habitat: walls, trees and woodland floor. Common throughout in suitable habitat.

Confusion plant: none.

Cow Parsley
Anthriscus sylvestris
Height: 40–150 cm
Heads: 3–8 cm, Apr–Jun
Erect plant with much-branched stems; slightly hairy; stem sometimes slightly purple. Tiny white flowers clustered into loose, irregularly shaped umbels. Fern-like and feathery leaves. Habitat: roadside verges, hedges and woodland rides. This is the most common umbellifer of spring, especially on roadsides.

Confusion plants: other umbellifers, for which a specialist guide may be necessary.

Wild Carrot
Daucus carota
Height: 20–100 cm
Heads: 2–10 cm, Jun–Sep
Hairy and erect-stemmed plant with branches often quite stout, and rarely achieving full height where it grows around the coast. Small white flowers occur in a flat-topped or dome-shaped head; often has a single, sterile, red flower in the centre. Fine, fern-like leaves are furry and smell of carrot when crushed. Habitat: meadows and coastal areas. Common throughout in suitable habitat.

Confusion plant: none.

Pignut
Conopodium majus
Height: 20–80 cm
Heads: 2.5–8 cm, May–Jul
A slender, hairless, delicate-looking umbellifer with a single stem. White and numerous flowers occurring in slightly domed heads. Upper leaves are thread-like. Habitat: hedges and open woodlands. Widespread, but not as common as many other umbellifers.

Confusion plant: Burnet Saxifrage, *Pimpinella saxifraga*, flowers May to September; has a downy stem; leaves more substantial, being fern-like rather than hair-like.

Wild Angelica
Angelica sylvestris
Height: 50–200 cm
Heads: 5–15 cm, Jul–Sep
Robust, almost hairless umbellifer; stout stems are hollow and often purplish. Tiny flowers are usually white, but sometimes pink, occurring in domed heads. Leaves divided two or three times into broad, toothed leaflets. Habitat: damp places, often next to streams or on marshy ground. Common throughout in suitable habitat.

Confusion plant: Garden Angelica, *Angelica archangelica*, has green stems and aromatic leaves; its flowers are often greenish-white.

Hogweed
Heracleum sphondylium
Height: 100–200 cm
Heads: Up to 25 cm, Jun–Oct
Erect, with stout, hairy stem, which is hollow. Flowers usually white, occasionally pink, occur in dense, flat-topped clusters, typical of umbellifers. Compound leaves deeply divided and toothed; coarsely hairy. Habitat: hedges, roadsides, waste ground and woodland edges. Common throughout in suitable habitat.

Confusion plant: Giant Hogweed, *Heracleum mantegazzianum*, is very rare, being found only near the Tamar; this is a huge plant often growing to 5 m tall.

Hemlock Water-dropwort
Oenanthe crocata
Height: 50–160 cm
Heads: 5–15 cm, Jun–Aug
An erect, much-branched plant without hairs; smells of parsley; poisonous; often grows in swathes in suitable habitat. Tiny white flowers occur in domed heads. Leaves split into many leaflets, each of which is toothed, resembling parsley leaves. Habitat: on damp ground by rivers and marshes. Common throughout in suitable habitat.

Confusion plant: none.

Rock Samphire
Crithmum maritimum
Height: 10–50 cm
Heads: 5–10 cm, Jun–Sep
A fleshy, hairless, sprawling plant with erect flower stems. Yellow-green, small flowers occur in dense, flattish-topped heads. Compound leaves with long, thin, fleshy leaflets. Habitat: rocky shores and coasts. Common throughout in suitable habitat.

Confusion plant: none.

Alexanders
Smyrnium olusatrum
Height: 50–150 cm
Heads: 5–15 cm, Mar–Jun
A leafy, hairless plant with stout, erect stems, and a yellowish-green appearance; common early in the year. Small yellow flowers are carried in domed heads. Leaves are trifoliate, glossy and toothed. Habitat: mostly hedges and roadsides. Common throughout in suitable habitat.

Confusion plant: none.

Heather (Ling)
Calluna vulgaris
Height: 20–60 cm
Flower: 0.3–0.4 cm, Aug–Oct
A woody-stemmed evergreen plant with erect stems and bushy manner. Flowers are tiny and pink but borne in impressive flower spikes. Tiny, scale-like leaves; dark green and very dry. Habitat: moorland and heathland. Common throughout in suitable habitat.

Confusion plant: none.

Bell Heather
Erica cinerea
Height: 15–75 cm
Flower: 0.4–0.8 cm, Jul–Sep
An evergreen, shrubby plant with tall flower spikes, woody stem and bushy appearance. Reddish-purple, bell-shaped flowers growing in clusters nod from the tops of stems. Small, pin-shaped leaves occur in whorls of three around the stems. Habitat: moorland and heathland. Common throughout in suitable habitat.

Confusion plant: none.

Cross-leaved Heath
Erica tetralix
Height: 15–60 cm
Flower: 0.4–0.8 cm, Jul–Sep
A downy-green, evergreen, straggling plant. Pale pink, bell-shaped flowers hang in clusters from the tops of stems in a nodding fashion. Leaves in whorls of four around the stem, hence the name 'cross-leaved'. Habitat: moorland and heathland. Common throughout in suitable habitat.

Confusion plant: Dorset Heath, *Erica ciliaris*, is rare in Cornwall and has larger, more elongated flowers and leaves in whorls of three; it can be found on Newlyn Downs.

Cornish Heath
Erica vagans
Height: 15–80 cm
Flower: 0.3–0.4 cm, Jul–Sep
A sprawling, evergreen shrub, quite robust looking. White or pink flowers have a chocolate-coloured rim and protruding anthers; flowers occur in robust circular flower spikes. Small, narrow leaves occur in whorls of four or five. Habitat: moorland and heathland. Restricted to the Lizard.

Confusion plant: none.

Bilberry
Vaccinium myrtillus
Height: 20–40 cm
Flower: 0.4–0.6 cm, Apr–Jul
A small shrub with woody, erect stems; distinctive and edible berry in summer. Flower is sac-like, looking like a berry, pink or greenish-pink. Leaves are bright green and oval. Habitat: moors, heaths and heathy woodland. Common throughout in suitable habitat.

Confusion plant: none.

Cowslip
Primula veris
Height: 5–20 cm
Flower: 0.8–2.5 cm, Apr–May
Erect flower stems from basal rosette of leaves, downy stem. The tubular-shaped yellow flowers have an orange spot at the centre; the flowers occur in a nodding, one-sided cluster at the tops of stems. The leaves are oval, but narrower at the base, toothed and wrinkled. Habitat: grassland, particularly dunes. Common, particularly on the north coast around Penhale, Polly Joke and Godrevy.

Confusion plant: none.

'Tisty-tosty, tell me true, Who shall I be married to?' This rhyme refers to a ball of cowslip flowers. Until the first half of the twentieth century, when cowslips were commoner, their flowers were wound into a ball of twine. The rhyme would continue with the names of possible spouses while throwing the ball into the air and catching it. If the ball landed on the ground, the future partner would be the last spoken name. Cowslips have been used in medicines; mixed with animal fat they made an ointment to cure bruises and cuts. One unusual name that refers to the overall shape of a cowslip is 'St Peter's Keys', which also reflects the importance of this plant to early Christians.

Yellow Loosestrife
Lysimachia vulgaris
Height: 40–150 cm
Flower: 1.5–2 cm, Jul–Sep
An erect, often patch-forming plant with downy leaves. Yellow flowers have five petals and are carried on short stalks in spike-shaped heads. The leaves are often black-dotted, occurring in opposite pairs. Habitat: hedgerows, damp meadows, riversides and waste ground. Common throughout in suitable habitat.

Confusion plant: none.

Primrose
Primula vulgaris
Height: 5–10 cm
Flower: 2–4 cm, Feb–Jun
A low, hairy plant forming clumps. The pale yellow flowers have five, notched petals and darker centres. The leaves are spoon-shaped, toothed and wrinkled. Habitat: woodland and hedges. Common throughout in suitable habitat.

Confusion plant: none.

Scarlet Pimpernel
Anagallis arvensis
Height: 5–50 cm
Flower: 0.3–0.8 cm, Apr–Oct
A creeping, prostrate, hairless plant. Pale scarlet or orange flowers with a darker centre; five petals; open in bright sunshine, closing when dull; occur on thin stems which grow in pairs from the main stem. Leaves are oval and in pairs from the main stem. Habitat: arable fields, dunes, grassland. Common throughout in suitable habitat.

Confusion plant: none.

Bog Pimpernel
Anagallis tenella
Height: 5–15 cm
Flower: 0.6–1 cm, Jun–Aug
Creeping, hairless, mat-forming plant. Bell-shaped, pale pink flower with darker veins; occur on thin stems which grow in pairs from main stem. Leaves are oval and small, occurring in pairs on short stems. Habitat: marshy ground. Widespread.

    Confusion plant: none.

Rock Sea-lavender
Limonium binervosum
Height: 10–50 cm
Flower: 0.4–0.8 cm, Jul–Sep
Woody stems are branched from near the base; stems erect, but plant has a sprawling habit often to avoid effects of strong wind and salt spray. Lilac-pink flowers are carried in spikes at the tips of each branch of the plant. Habitat: coastal, particularly on rocky areas. Widespread but not common.

    Confusion plants: there are many sub-species of rock sea lavender.

Bogbean
Menyanthes trifoliata
Height: 20–40 cm
Flower: 1.2–1.7 cm, Apr–Jul
An aquatic plant which stands proud of the water, forming patches at the edge of open water. Flowers are white with pink tinges, star-shaped and fringed with dense white hairs. The long-stalked, trifoliate leaves are held above the water. Habitat: marshes and freshwater pools. Uncommon, can be found on Goss Moor.

    Confusion plant: none.

Thrift (Sea Pink)

Armeria maritima
Height: 5–20 cm
Heads: 1–3 cm, Apr–Sep
Low growing, forming densely packed, springy mounds; slightly downy stems. Tiny pink (occasionally white) flowers grow in tightly packed, spherical heads on top of flexible but erect stems. Thin, grass-like leaves. Habitat: coastal, particularly rocky areas, also sandy soils. Common throughout in suitable habitat.

Confusion plant: none.

Thrift is one of the most distinctive flowers of the Cornish coastline; it also prospers on old mining waste. Folklore suggests you will never be poor if thrift grows in your garden. In fact, it is likely that the name 'thrift' was derived from the same roots as the word 'thrive', and the plant certainly does thrive around the coast of the county.

Fringed Water-lily
Nymphoides peltata
Height: Up to 150 cm
Flower: 3–4 cm, Jun–Sep
An aquatic plant with floating leaves and flowers. Flowers are yellow and have five petals which are fringed. The leaves are kidney-shaped, almost circular and float. Habitat: freshwater lakes and ponds. Uncommon, Bissoe is good for this species.

Confusion plant: none.

Common Centaury
Centaurium erythraea
Height: 5–30 cm
Flower: 0.5–0.8 cm, Jun–Oct
A hairless plant, very variable in size according to habitat: tall and slender inland, and quite short near the coast. Flowers are pink; tubular with the fringe forming five lobes; occurring in flat-topped clusters. Leaves are oval at base of plant, narrower along stem. Habitat: dry grassland, especially dunes and coastal areas. Common throughout in suitable habitat.

Confusion plant: none.

Field Gentian
Gentianella campestris
Height: 10–30 cm
Flower: 1–2 cm, Jun–Oct
An erect, branched, hairless plant. Bluish-purple, funnel-shaped flowers with four petal-like lobes, contained within a sepal tube. Oval leaves occur in opposite pairs from stem. Habitat: grassland and dunes. Rare, good places include Kit Hill and the Lizard.

Confusion plant: Autumn Gentian (Felwort), *Gentianella amarella*, has purple flowers; and Early Gentian, *Gentianella anglica*, flowers May to June and has five-lobed flowers; both occur in Cornwall.

Common Dodder

Cuscuta epithymum
Height: 5–50 cm
Flower: 0.3–0.4 cm, Jul–Sep
A climbing, entwining parasitic plant without roots; its red stems form a net over its host species, usually gorse. Small and pink flowers form clusters of up to about 1 cm across. It has scale-like and extremely small leaves. Habitat: anywhere that gorse occurs, often coastal. Common throughout in suitable habitat.

Confusion plant: none.

The common dodder belongs to the same family as bindweed, and shares its climbing habit, but that is where the similarities end. Dodder is exceptional among British plants in being a stem parasite. Dodder takes its nutrients from the host plants through tiny, root-like structures that penetrate into their conducting tissue. One of its favourite hosts is gorse, and that is why its distribution in Cornwall is often coastal. The sprawling mats of dodder can look quite sinister and this, no doubt, contributed to it being called 'hellweed' and 'devil's guts'.

√ Cape Cornwall 6/18

Hedge Bindweed (Bellbine)

Calystegia sepium
Height: 100–300 cm
Flower: 3–6 cm, Jun–Sep
Hairless climber, has many stems growing from an underground rhizome; stem twines around other vegetation, anticlockwise. Large white, rarely pink, trumpet-shaped flowers; the bracts, behind the flower, are large but do not overlap. Large, heart-shaped leaves arranged alternately along the stem. Habitat: hedges, fields, riversides, woodland edges, scrub. Extremely common.

Confusion plant: Large Bindweed, *Calystegia silvatica*, has larger flowers (6–7 cm across) and overlapping bracts.

Field Bindweed (Bellbine)

Convolvulus arvensis
Height: 50–200 cm
Flower: 1.5–3 cm, May–Sep
An often downy, creeping or twining plant. Trumpet-shaped, white and pink flowers occasionally occurring in pairs. Leaves can be oval, spear-shaped or triangular. Habitat: arable fields and waste ground. Widespread but local due to habitat requirements, West Pentire is good.

Confusion plant: Sea Bindweed, *Calystegia soldanella*, which has a larger flower (3–5 cm), kidney-shaped, fleshy leaves, and grows by the coast.

Field Madder

Sherardia arvensis
Height: 10–40 cm
Flower: 0.2–0.3 cm, May–Sep
A sprawling, hairy plant. The flowers are pale purple, funnel-shaped with four lobes, occurring in heads surrounded by leaf-like bracts. The leaves are hairy, narrow and pointed, occurring in whorls around the stem. Habitat: arable fields and some grassland. Common throughout in suitable habitat.

Confusion plant: none.

Wild Madder
Rubia peregrina
Height: 30–120 cm
Flower: 0.4–0.6 cm, Jun–Aug
A slightly woody, scrambling and climbing plant. The tiny, yellowish-green flowers are funnel shaped and have five petal lobes. The leaves are narrowly oval and prickly for climbing; they occur in whorls of four to six. Habitat: woodland, scrub and waste ground. Uncommon.

Confusion plant: none.

Goosegrass (Cleavers)
Galium aparine
Height: 50–200 cm
Flower: 0.2–0.3 cm, May–Sep
A climbing or scrambling plant with square stems, and covered in soft, curved prickles which stick to clothing and animal fur. White, funnel-shaped flowers have four lobes. Narrow leaves occur in whorls of between six and nine leaflets. Habitat: hedges, scrub and woodland. Common throughout in suitable habitat.

Confusion plant: none.

Hedge Bedstraw
Galium album
Height: 20–140 cm
Flower: 0.2–0.3 cm, Jun–Sep
A scrambling plant with square, hairy stems. Tiny white flowers are funnel shaped and carried in loose clusters. Elliptical leaves grow in whorls of six to eight leaflets around the stem. Habitat: hedges, grassland and woodland. Common throughout in suitable habitat.

Confusion plant: Heath Bedstraw, *Galium saxatile*, is more prostrate, shorter with less flamboyant flower clusters, and occurs on heathland.

Field Forget-me-not
Myosotis arvensis
Height: 5–25 cm
Flower: 0.3–0.5 cm, May–Sep
Small, erect, greyish-coloured plant. Pale blue flowers have five petals and a yellow centre; occur in spikes which lengthen as the plant grows. Leaves oval and hairy, those at the base forming a basal rosette. Habitat: particularly arable fields, also waste ground, other disturbed soils. Common throughout in suitable habitat.

Confusion plant: Water Forget-me-not, *Myosotis scorpioides*, grows in and beside streams, has slightly notched petals; Wood Forget-me-not, *Myosotis sylvatica*, has larger flowers (0.6–1 cm) and occurs in woods and gardens.

Lady's Bedstraw
Galium verum
Height: 10–80 cm
Flower: 0.2–0.3 cm, May–Sep
A sprawling plant with hairy stems, some of which are erect. Tiny, funnel-shaped, yellow flowers are sweetly scented (was once used to scent hay mattresses), and occur in dense clusters. Leaves are narrow and occur in whorls of between eight and 12 leaflets around the stem. Habitat: sand dunes and grassland. Common throughout in suitable habitat.

Confusion plant: none

Comfrey
Symphytum officinale
Height: 40–130 cm
Flower: 1.2–2 cm, May–Jul
An erect, hairy plant with branched stems. Flower colour variable, including reddish-purple, white and blue; flowers are tubular in shape, and occur in nodding, one-sided clusters. Leaves spear-shaped; those on the stems merge with the stem to create 'wings'. Various habitats including hedges, riversides and waste ground. Common.

Confusion plant: none.

Viper's Bugloss
Echium vulgare
Height: 20–90 cm
Flower: 1.5–2 cm, May–Sep
Very tall and erect, often with many stems from a basal rosette of leaves; distinctive pattern of dark scales on the stem. Flowers start pink and turn blue; funnel-shaped with protruding red stamens; grow on curving stems at the sides of the main stem. Leaves spear-shaped with rough hairs; lack prominent side veins. Habitat: waste ground and particularly sand dunes. Common throughout in suitable habitat.

Confusion plant: Purple Viper's Bugloss, *Echium plantagineum*, flower colour and habitat should clinch identity.

Bugloss
Anchusa arvensis
Height: 10–50 cm
Flower: 0.4–0.6 cm, Apr–Sep
Bristly with erect stem. Flower is blue with five joined petals and a paler centre, growing in elongating clusters. Wavy-edged, bristly leaves. Habitat: disturbed ground such as arable fields. Uncommon, a good location is West Pentire.

Confusion plants: Alkanet, *Anchusa officinalis*, has bluish-purple flowers and is more softly hairy; Green Alkanet, *Pentaglottis sempervirens*, is a flower of woods and hedges.

Borage
Borago officinalis
Height: 15–70 cm
Flower: 2–3 cm, May–Sep
Erect and bristly with arching sprays of flowers. Flowers are blue with five petals, which tend to curve back from the prominent stamens; they occur in clusters. The leaves are roughly oval and bristly, with wavy margins. Habitat: disturbed ground such as arable fields. Common throughout in suitable habitat.

Confusion plant: none.

Purple Viper's Bugloss
Echium plantagineum
Height: 20–70 cm
Flower: 2.5–3 cm, May–Jul
Tall, hairy plant often growing *en masse*. Flowers vary from red to purple; funnel-shaped; many flowers grow from the top of each curving stem; has protruding red stamens. Leaves have prominent side veins. Habitat: a weed of arable fields. Rare, the best location is Boscregan Farm.

Confusion plant: Viper's Bugloss, *Echium vulgare*, flower colour and habitat should clinch identification.

Purple viper's bugloss is more at home in the Mediterranean climate since it flourishes in warmer parts of the world. In Australia it has become a pest species, known as Patterson's curse. The purple viper's bugloss was first recorded at Boscregan Farm, where it still grows in profusion, in 1873, but it may have existed there for much longer, since trading between Cornwall and mainland Europe dates back millennia. Here it grows among barley and corn marigolds, making a wonderful combination of colours and shapes.

Green Alkanet
Pentaglottis sempervirens
Height: 20–60 cm
Flower: 0.8–1 cm, Apr–Jul
An erect, roughly hairy plant with large leaves and small blue flowers. Blue flower with white centre. Pointed, oval leaves with hairs. Habitat: woods and hedges. Common throughout in suitable habitat.

Confusion plant: Bugloss, *Anchusa arvensis*, has wavy-edged leaves and grows in arable fields.

Bugle
Ajuga reptans
Height: 10–30 cm
Flower: 1.4–1.7 cm, Apr–Jun
A creeping plant with many short, dark, hairy flower spikes on square stems. Flower is dark purple/blue, tubular with large lower lip, occurring in whorls around the stem. Leaves occur in opposite pairs around the stem; hairy and often tinted bronze. Habitat: damp woodland and grass-land. Common throughout in suitable habitat.

Confusion plant: Skullcap, *Scutellaria galericulata*, has flowers in pairs not whorls; its leaves are more pointed.

Skullcap
Scutellaria galericulata
Height: 10–50 cm
Flower: 1–2 cm, Jun–Sep
An erect, downy plant with a square stem. The bluish-purple flowers are tubular, each has a white spot on the lower lip, and they are borne in pairs from the leafy stem. The leaves are spear-shaped and occur in opposite pairs. Habitat: wet, grassy places. Widespread.

Confusion plant: Bugle, *Ajuga reptans*, has flowers occurring in whorls around the stem.

Wood Sage

Teucrium scorodonia
Height: 20–60 cm
Flower: 0.7–1 cm, Jun–Oct
An erect plant, quite woody, with square stem. The flowers are greenish-cream, sometimes marked with red; they are borne in leafless spikes. The leaves are heart-shaped, toothed and wrinkled. Habitat: heaths and woodland, particularly dry areas. Common throughout in suitable habitat.

Confusion plant: none.

Ground Ivy

Glechoma hederacea
Height: 10–40 cm
Flower: 1.5–2.5 cm, Mar–Jun
A creeping and partly erect plant which is softly hairy and often purple tinged; aromatic. Flowers are violet-blue and tubular in shape, occurring in whorls around the stem. The leaves are kidney shaped and toothed. Habitat: hedges, woodland and grassland. Common throughout in suitable habitat.

Confusion plant: none.

Self-heal

Prunella vulgaris
Height: 5–50 cm
Flower: 1–1.5 cm, Jun–Nov
A prostrate plant with erect flower stems; hairy and square-stemmed. The flowers are deep purple, very occasionally pink or even white; they are carried in compact, cylindrical heads with hairy, leaf-like bracts. The leaves are oval, and occur in opposite pairs. Habitat: woodland, grassland, hedges and gardens. Common throughout in suitable habitat.

Confusion plant: none.

Yellow Archangel
Lamiastrum galeobdolon
subsp. *argentatum*
Height: 20–50 cm
Flower: 1.5–2.5 cm, Apr–Jul
An erect, square-stemmed plant with runners which quickly establish large patches. Flowers are yellow with reddish-brown markings on the lower lip; they occur in whorls around the stem. Leaves are oval or spear-shaped with toothed edges. Habitat: hedges and woodland. Common throughout in suitable habitat.

Confusion plant: similar form to the White Dead-nettle, *Lamium album*, from which it varies in flower colour.

White Dead-nettle
Lamium album
Height: 20–80 cm
Flower: 1.8–2.5 cm, Mar–Nov
An erect plant with square, hairy stems. The flowers are creamy white and occur in whorls around the stem. The leaves are heart-shaped with toothed edges; they do not sting. Habitat: hedges, roadsides and waste ground. Common throughout in suitable habitat.

Confusion plants: similar in form to the Yellow Archangel, *Lamiastrum galeobdolon*; there is also a Red Dead-nettle, *Lamium purpureum*, which has reddish-purple flowers.

Betony
Stachys officinalis
Height: 10–100 cm
Flower: 1.2–1.8 cm, Jun–Oct
An erect plant with hairy, square, unbranched stems. The flowers are reddish-purple and are borne in a loose flower spike. Leaves are narrow, toothed, and occur in opposite pairs on the stem. Particularly common around the coast, also around hedges, waste ground and woodland edges. Common throughout in suitable habitat.

Confusion plant: none.

Marsh Woundwort
Stachys palustris
Height: 50–120 cm
Flower: 1.2–1.8 cm, Jun–Oct
An erect plant, roughly hairy with square stems. Flowers are pinkish-purple with white patterning; they grow in whorls on a tall flower spike. Leaves are narrow and pointed, coarsely toothed, faintly smelling and occur in opposite pairs. Habitat: marshy ground, ditches, etc. Common throughout in suitable habitat.

Confusion plant: Hedge Woundwort, *Stachys sylvatica*, has reddish-purple flowers and broader, more aromatic leaves; it is found in hedges and woodland.

Water Mint
Mentha aquatica
Height: 20–70 cm
Flower: 0.3–0.4 cm, Jul–Oct
Hairy, with erect, often purplish, stems. Flowers are pale lilac, borne in dense heads at the tops of the stems. Leaves oval, but pointed at the tip and toothed; occur in opposite pairs and are aromatic. Habitat: marshy ground. Common throughout in suitable habitat.

Confusion plant: Corn Mint, *Mentha arvensis*, has flowers in whorls around stem, not at the top of stem; Spear Mint, *Mentha spicata*, has pointed flower spike; Pennyroyal, *Mentha pulegium*, has flowers like Corn Mint, much smaller leaves which are not toothed.

Wild Thyme
Thymus polytrichus
Height: 5–10 cm
Flower: 0.3–0.4 cm, May–Sep
An aromatic, mat-forming plant with slightly woody stems. The flowers are pink and have a three-lobed lower lip, they are borne in spherical heads but these merge into a mass of flowers. The leaves are oval and occur in opposite pairs. Habitat: particularly sand dunes and rocky coastlines. Common throughout in suitable habitat.

Confusion plant: none.

Common Figwort
Scrophularia nodosa
Height: 40–100 cm
Flower: 0.8–1.2 cm, Jun–Sep
Hairless, with erect, square stems. Small, helmet-shaped flowers have a wine-red upper lip and green lower lip. Leaves spear-shaped, toothed and unpleasantly smelling. Habitat: woodlands and hedges in shady places. Common throughout in suitable habitat.

Confusion plants: Water Figwort, *Scrophularia nodosa*, has blunter leaves, winged stems, and grows in wetter places; Balm-leaved Figwort, *Scrophularia scorodonia*, has heart-shaped leaves and red-brown flowers; grows in sandy places likes Scilly and West Pentire.

Bittersweet (Woody Nightshade)
Solanum dulcamara
Height: 50–200 cm
Flower: 1.2–1.7 cm, May–Oct
A climbing plant with a downy, woody stem; the red berries are obvious in late summer; poisonous. The five-petalled flowers are deep purple with a prominent set of yellow anthers. The leaves are spear-shaped. Habitat: shady places such as hedges and woodland. Common throughout in suitable habitat.

Confusion plant: none.

Black Nightshade
Solanum nigrum
Height: 10–50 cm
Flower: 0.6–1 cm, Jul–Nov
A downy plant with erect, much-branched, often blackish, stems; black berries are poisonous. The flowers are whitish with yellow anthers. The leaves are oval but pointed. Habitat: a weed of arable fields. Common throughout in suitable habitat.

Confusion plant: none.

√ St Mary's 6/18

Great Mullein

Verbascum thapsus
Height: 80–200 cm
Flower: 2–3.5 cm, Jun–Sep
A tall, erect, robust, leafy plant with a white, almost felted downy covering. The flowers are pale yellow with five petals. The leaves are large and oval or spear-shaped. Habitat: waste ground, sunny banks and scrub. Common throughout in suitable habitat.

Confusion plants: Dark Mullein, *Verbascum nigrum*, is hairy but lacks the white woolly texture; Moth Mullein, *Verbascum blattaria* and Twiggy Mullein, *Verbascum virgatum*, have separate flowers on short stalks, and shiny leaves.

Ivy-leaved Toadflax

Cymbalaria muralis
Height: 10–70 cm
Flower: 1–1.5 cm, Apr–Nov
A trailing plant; hairless with a reddish-purple tinge to the stem and leaves. The flowers are usually lilac in colour with a yellow central patch; they grow on stalks. The leaves are approximately kidney-shaped with shallow lobes, a little like an ivy leaf. It is often found on walls, but also on gravel and rocks. Common throughout in suitable habitat.

Confusion plant: none.

Common Toadflax

Linaria vulgaris
Height: 20–70 cm
Flower: 2–3 cm, Jun–Nov
Erect plant with greyish-green, hairy and leafy stems which grow in clumps. The flowers are pale yellow with a deeper coloured centre, carried in densely packed flower spikes. The leaves are very narrow and crowd the stem. Habitat: hedgerows, roadsides, gardens and waste ground. Common throughout in suitable habitat.

Confusion plant: none.

Foxglove

Digitalis purpurea
Height: 50–200 cm
Flower: 3–5 cm, May–Sep
Erect, unbranched plant with very tall flower spikes. The flowers are pink with purple and white spots inside the flower tube, where there are also hairs. The spear-shaped leaves occur around the base of the plant, and are softly hairy. Habitat: woods, scrub, hedges. Common throughout in suitable habitat.

Confusion plant: none.

The name foxglove wasn't originally derived from the fox. The flower was likened to a glove belonging to the little folk – 'folk's glove' – but was corrupted to the more popular variation. The foxglove is extremely poisonous, though it can be used in medicine for certain heart problems. Despite its toxicity, children once played with the flowers, inflating and popping them. Growing foxgloves in the garden is supposed to keep evil at bay, so there are now many colour variants in gardens (left).

Lesser Snapdragon (Weaselsnout)
Misopates orontium
Height: 10–50 cm
Flower: 1–1.5 cm, Jul–Oct
A short, downy, erect plant. The flowers are pink with a white centre and some darker veining. The leaves are narrowly oval and downy. Habitat: arable fields. Uncommon, West Pentire and Boscregan are good locations.

Confusion plant: none.

Yellow Bartsia
Parentucellia viscosa
Height: 20–70 cm
Flower: 1.6–2.4 cm, Jun–Sep
An erect plant with sticky hairs; this is a semi-parasitic species. The flowers are yellow and hooded with a lower lip split into three lobes. The leaves are narrow and spear-shaped, occurring in opposite pairs and toothed. Habitat: a variety of grassy places including dunes. Fairly common.

Confusion plant: Red Bartsia, *Odontites vernus*, is similar but with pinkish-red flowers and often purplish stems.

✓ St Mary's
6/18

Germander Speedwell
Veronica chamaedrys
Height: 10–30 cm
Flower: 0.8–1.2 cm, Apr–Jul
A hairy, semi-erect plant sprawling through grasses. The flowers have four blue lobes, of which the lowest is the smallest, with a white centre; they are carried in spikes arising in opposite pairs from the stem; the two stamens are obvious, having white pollen at the ends. The leaves are heart-shaped, toothed and wrinkled. Habitat: any grassy places in woods, near hedges, or in gardens. Very common.

Confusion plant: many other speedwells, for which a specialist guide is necessary.

Heath Speedwell
Veronica officinalis
Height: 10–30 cm
Flower: 0.6–0.8 cm, May–Aug
A low, creeping, hairy plant with short, upright flower stems. Flowers are lilac-blue with dark veins; they are four-lobed, with the lower lobe the smallest and upper the largest; borne in spikes which are usually pyramidal in shape. The leaves are in opposite pairs, toothed and broadly oval in shape. Habitat: dry grassland, heaths and sometimes waste ground. Fairly common.

Confusion plant: many other speedwells, for which a specialist guide is necessary.

Slender Speedwell
Veronica filiformis
Height: 5–20 cm
Flower: 1–1.5 cm, Apr–Jun
A low, sprawling, mat-forming, downy plant originally introduced as a garden plant. The flowers are solitary, growing on long stalks; their top half is blue and their bottom half is white, shows darker veins and a white eye. The leaves are heart shaped and toothed. Habitat: grassland and gardens. Common.

Confusion plant: many other speedwells, for which a specialist guide is necessary.

Common Cow-wheat
Melampyrum pratense
Height: 20–60 cm
Flower: 1–2 cm, May–Sep
An erect but slightly flimsy plant. The flowers are pale yellow and tube-like, but flattened, occurring in a single-sided spike. Narrowly oval leaves occur in opposite pairs. Habitat: heath and woodland. Uncommon.

Confusion plant: nearest similar plant is Yellow Rattle, *Rhinanthus minor*, which should be easily distinguished.

Eyebright

Euphrasia officinalis
Height: 5–20 cm
Flower: 0.5–1 cm, Jun–Oct

A tiny, upright plant; dark green and stickily hairy; semi-parasitic. The flowers are white, striped with purple, and with a yellow spot in the centre of the lower lip. The leaves are oval with toothed edges and lacking stems. Habitat: grassland, particularly dunes. Common throughout in suitable habitat.

Confusion plant: none.

Eyebright's flowers are regularly self-pollinated, thus encouraging distinctive local characteristics, and so eyebright has become one of our most variable flowering plants. However, one consistent feature of its flower, the yellow spot in the centre of the large lower petal, obviously evolved to attract insects. This spot serves as a landing pad for bees, indicating the position of the nectar, and tempting the insect to come into contact with the pollen-bearing anthers. Through history, plants have been used as medicines, and often they were chosen on the basis that they looked like the subject of the ailment! Eyebright, with its distinctive yellow 'eye' was therefore used to treat eye conditions, particularly inflamed eyelids and conjunctivitis. It is now known that some of its ingredients are active in the inhibition of bacteria. Although eyebright is green, and so does contain chlorophyll, it doesn't produce all of its own nutrients; instead it is semi-parasitic, taking some nutrients from the roots of the grasses with which it associates.

Lousewort
Pedicularis sylvatica
Height: 10–20 cm
Flower: 1.5–2.5 cm, Apr–Aug
Sprawling, but with semi-erect stems; a semi-parasitic plant. The flower is pink, its upper lip longer than the lower, with an enlarged brown sepal tube. It has small, deeply cut leaves, dark green with a purplish tinge. Habitat: heathland, moorland and bogs. Common throughout in suitable habitat.

Confusion plant: Marsh Lousewort, *Pedicularis palustris*, has a redder-coloured flower, in which the two lips are roughly equal in length; also has a hairier sepal tube.

Yellow Rattle
Rhinanthus minor
Height: 10–40 cm
Flower: 1–1.5 cm, May–Aug
Erect plant with longish stems, without many leaves; stems often brown or reddish; when in seed can be rattled; a semi-parasitic species. Yellow, two-lipped flower within an inflated sepal tube. Narrow, pointed and toothed leaves, occurring in opposite pairs. Habitat: grassland, particularly dunes. Common throughout in suitable habitat.

Confusion plant: see Common Cow-wheat, *Melampyrum pratense*.

Thyme Broomrape
Orobanche alba
Height: 5–40 cm
Flower: 1.5–2.5 cm, May–Aug
An erect flower spike with very small leaves; red all over, soon changing to rusty brown as the plant dies; parasitic on Wild Thyme. The tubular-shaped flowers are red, hairy and scented. The scale-like leaves are narrow and grow only from the stem. Habitat: grassland around the coast. Uncommon, one good location is around Kynance Cove.

Confusion plants: other broomrapes, see Common Broomrape, *Orobanche minor*.

Common Broomrape
Orobanche minor
Height: 10–50 cm
Flower: 1–1.5 cm, May–Sep
An erect flower spike, showing no green because it is parasitic, often found on wild carrot, or the pea and daisy families. Flowers brownish-yellow, often tinged red or purple; each tubular in shape. Leaves scale-like around the stem. Habitat: usually dry grassland, sometimes coastal, occasionally waste ground. Fairly common.

Confusion plants: many other broomrapes, mostly parasitic on a specific species, such as: Knapweed Broomrape, *Orobanche elatior*; Yarrow Broomrape, *Orobanche purpurea*; Bedstraw Broomrape, *Orobanche caryophyllacea*.

Ribwort Plantain
Plantago lanceolata
Height: 20–60 cm
Flower: Tiny, Apr–Oct
A plant with stout, erect, ridged stems. The flowers are brown and very small, borne in packed cylindrical clusters at the tops of stems. The leaves are long and pointed, with heavy veining. Habitat: grassland and waste ground. Common throughout in suitable habitat.

Confusion plant: none.

Red Valerian
Centranthus ruber
Height: 40–80 cm
Flower: 0.5–1 cm, Jun–Sep
Semi-erect, clump-forming; grey-green stems and hairless. The flowers are pink, white or red and are carried in large, branched clusters. The leaves are pointed, and in pairs around the stem. It often grows on ruined walls, banks, rocks, and cliffs where it is dry. Common throughout in suitable habitat.

Confusion plant: none.

Common Valerian
Valeriana officinalis
Height: 50–200 cm
Flower: 0.3–0.5 cm, Jun–Aug
Hairy and thin-stemmed, but quite robust and tall. Pale pink flowers occur in small clusters at the tops of tall stems. The leaves occur in opposite pairs, and are compound or deeply lobed. Habitat: woodland glades, meadows, marshy ground. Common throughout in suitable habitat.

Confusion plant: none.

Honeysuckle
Lonicera periclymenum
Height: 100–600 cm
Flower: 3–8 cm, May–Oct
A woody climber twining clockwise. The tubular flowers are yellow and sweetly scented, borne in whorled clusters at the tips of the branches. The oval, slightly downy leaves are borne in pairs. Habitat: woodland, hedgerows and coastal. Common throughout in suitable habitat.

Confusion plant: none.

Hemp Agrimony
Eupatorium cannabinum
Height: 30–180 cm
Flower: 0.3–0.5 cm, Jul–Oct
Tall, erect plant with reddish stems and downy texture. Many small, pink flowers form flattish-topped, rather untidy-looking clusters. The leaves occur in opposite pairs, and are spear-shaped with toothed edges. Habitat: hedges, waste ground, scrub, woodland. Common throughout in suitable habitat.

Confusion plant: none.

Teasel

Dipsacus fullonum
Height: 50–220 cm
Heads: 5–10 cm, Jun–Sep

A strong, erect plant with spiny stems. Small, pinkish-purple flowers grow from a prickly teasel-head. The leaves grow in opposite, fused pairs which often hold water near the stem; they have a row of prickles underneath. Habitat: waste ground, hedges, and where fields become overgrown. Common throughout in suitable habitat.

Confusion plant: none.

The teasel is a very useful plant for encouraging wildlife in the garden. In summer its flowers are attractive to bees, and in early autumn its seeds are eaten by goldfinches. Its unusual leaves hold a reservoir of water by the stem, and this water was once used as a cosmetic for cleansing the skin, and even the eyes.

Sheepsbit Scabious (Sheepsbit)
Jasione montana
Height: 10–40 cm
Heads: 1–2.5 cm, May–Sep
A small, erect, hairy plant often forming clumps. Small blue flowers make up hemispherical heads, which look a bit untidy. Leaves are narrow, and sometimes have a wavy edge. Habitat: mostly coastal on rocky areas. Common throughout in suitable habitat.

Confusion plant: this is actually a bellflower, not a scabious, but its only possible confusion species is the Devilsbit Scabious, *Succisa pratensis*, which is much taller and branched, with very neat, more purplish, hemispherical heads.

Field Scabious
Knautia arvensis
Height: 30–100 cm
Heads: 2–4 cm, Jul–Oct
A tall, erect, hairy plant with branches. The flowers are lilac in colour, and make up a flattish-topped, compound head in which the central flowers are smaller than the outer ones. The leaves occur in opposite pairs, and are spear-shaped with lobes. Habitat: hedges, grassland, dunes and roadsides. Common throughout in suitable habitat.

Confusion plant: none.

Devilsbit Scabious
Succisa pratensis
Height: 20–110 cm
Heads: 2–2.5 cm, Jul–Oct
An erect plant, with tall stems and branches. Purple flowers form a neat, hemispherical head, growing at the tops of the tall stems. The leaves are oval and quite narrow; the largest leaves occur as a basal rosette; higher up the stems the leaves are small and insignificant. Habitat: damp grassland. Widespread.

Confusion plant: Sheepsbit Scabious, *Jasione montana*, is much shorter, and with bluer, less neat-looking flowers.

Golden Samphire
Inula crithmoides
Height: 10–70 cm
Flower: 2–2.5 cm, Jul–Oct
A fleshy, erect plant. Flowers are daisy-like but completely yellow. Leaves are linear and fleshy, sometimes with three teeth and the tip. Habitat: coastal on rocks and saltmarsh. Uncommon.

Confusion plant: none.

Golden-rod
Solidago virgaurea
Height: 30–180 cm
Flower: 0.5–1 cm, Jun–Sep
A tall, stout plant with downy stems. The flowers are yellow with outer ray florets, a little like those of ragwort, borne in spikes. The leaves along the stem are spear-shaped and slightly toothed. Habitat: heaths, hedges and dry woodland. Common.

Confusion plant: this species is vaguely reminiscent of Common Ragwort, *Senecio jacobaea*, which has flowers in flat-topped clusters.

Daisy
Bellis perennis
Height: 5–20 cm
Flower: 1–3 cm, Jan–Dec
Small, familiar flower of lawns; each hairy stem has one flower at the top. Disc florets of flower are yellow; ray florets are white, sometimes reddish underneath. Spoon-shaped leaves occur at the base of the plant. Habitat: lawns and other grassy areas. Common throughout in suitable habitat.

Confusion plant: none, but mayweeds and oxeye daisies have similar flowers.

Pineapple Mayweed (Pineapple Weed)

Matricaria discoidea
Height: 10–30 cm
Flower: 0.5–1 cm, May–Nov
A hairless, much-branched, bushy plant. Greenish-yellow flowers are like a daisy, but without the outer white ray florets. The leaves are thread-like. Habitat: waste ground, arable fields, pathsides and hedges. Common throughout in suitable habitat.

Confusion plant: None.

Scentless Mayweed

Tripleurospermum inodorum
Height: 10–70 cm
Flower: 2–4 cm, Apr–Nov
Semi-erect, many branches. Daisy-like flowers, but much larger, with a slightly bulbous head. Feathery leaves. Habitat: arable fields, waste ground and roadsides. Common throughout in suitable habitat.

Confusion plants: Sea Mayweed, *Tripleurospermum maritimum*, is stouter, slightly fleshy, and occurs by the sea; Scented Mayweed, *Matricaria recutita*, is aromatic, and has down-turned white outer ray florets.

Common Fleabane

Pulicaria dysenterica
Height: 20–60 cm
Flower: 1.5–3 cm, Jul–Oct
A hairy, erect plant forming patches; has woolly, whit-ish stems and leaves. Daisy-like flowers, but with yellow outer ray florets. The leaves are spear shaped with a wavy edge. Habitat: grassland, par-ticularly in damp areas. Com-mon throughout in suitable habitat.

Confusion plant: Elecam-pane, *Inula helenium*, has much larger flowers (6–8 cm).

Yarrow

Achillea millefolium
Height: 20–80 cm
Flower: 0.4–0.6 cm, Jun–Nov
Hairy-stemmed, erect plant often forming clumps, quite aromatic. Flower is small, usually white but sometimes pink. Flowers occur in tightly packed, flat-topped, often irregularly shaped clusters. Leaves are split into tiny, feathery form, hence the scientific name *millefolium*. Habitat: varied, including grassland and wasteland. Common throughout in suitable habitat.

Confusion plant: Sneezewort, *Achillea ptarmica*, has larger flowers which do not form a flat-topped head.

Yarrow is a flower with a great medicinal pedigree. Its scientific name, *Achillea millefolium*, hints at its early importance to humankind as it is named after the Greek hero Achilles; *millefolium* is a reference to its very finely divided leaves. Among its repertoire of remedies, yarrow was used to cure gastric problems, including flatulence; rheumatism; bronchitis; coughs and colds; to stop nosebleeds; cure headaches; to assist in the production of bile, and as a tranquilizer. It was also used as an astringent for wounds, and one of its alternative names, Carpenter's Herb, came into being because carpenters often used it to heal wounds after cutting themselves in their work. Not only was it used for humans, but also for cattle and, as is so often the case, recent scientific analysis has revealed several elements in yarrow which do indeed act as tranquilizers and have antibacterial effects.

Sneezewort
Achillea ptarmica
Height: 30–100 cm
Flower: 1.2–1.5 cm, Jul–Sep
Hairy-stemmed, erect plant, not aromatic. Flower is white with a creamy/grey centre, occurring in loose clusters. Long and thin leaves, hugging stem slightly, fine saw-toothed edge. Habitat: acidic, damp soils. Widespread but not common.

Confusion plant: Yarrow, *Achillea millefolium*, has smaller flowers which form a flat-topped head.

Mugwort
Artemisia vulgaris
Height: 50–160 cm
Flower: 0.2–0.3 cm, Jul–Sep
Scruffy, greyish plant with tough, erect, downy stem; aromatic. Flowers are egg-shaped, yellowish or reddish brown, occurring in branched spikes. Leaves are green above and silvery-grey below, deeply lobed with heavily toothed edges. Habitat: waste ground and roadsides. Common throughout in suitable habitat.

Confusion plant: Worm-wood, *Artemesia absinthium*, is strongly aromatic; upper leaf surface is whiter and downy.

Winter Heliotrope
Petasites fragrans
Height: 15–25 cm
Heads: 3–6 cm, Nov–Mar
A plant which forms extensive patches with its huge leaves covering the ground. The flowers are white or pinkish, with outer ray florets held in a shaving-brush shape; many of these grow in a roughly domed cluster. The large leaves are heart-shaped and rough. Habitat: woodlands and waste ground. Common throughout in suitable habitat.

Confusion plant: Butterbur, *Petasites hybridus*, has huge leaves (up to 1 m across), and a greater number of pinkish flowers in each head.

Corn Marigold
Bothams (Scilly)
Chrysanthemum segetum
Height: 15–80 cm
Flower: 3.5–5.5 cm, Jun–Oct
Erect or semi-erect plant, with a bluish-green tinge; quite fleshy. Flowers have a yellow disc with prominent yellow ray florets; occurring singly at the end of stems. Leaves deeply toothed, particularly around base of plant. Habitat: arable fields. Where conditions are suitable is very common, but locally distributed; West Pentire, Boscregan and St Mary's (Scilly) are excellent for this species.

Confusion plant: none.

Oxeye Daisy
Leucanthemum vulgare
Height: 20–100 cm
Flower: 2.5–5 cm, May–Oct
An erect plant with little branching along its stems. Flowers are like daisies, but larger. The leaves are dark green, all are lobed, and upper leaves hug the stem. Found on roadside verges where it has been introduced; the native varieities can still be found around the coast, and these are much shorter than the introduced types. Common throughout in suitable habitat.

Confusion plant: none.

Feverfew
(Bachelor's Buttons)
Tanacetum parthenium
Height: 20–80 cm
Flower: 1–2 cm, Jun–Sep
An erect plant with much branching; highly aromatic with downy stem. Daisy-like flowers, but with relatively short white outer ray florets; flowers are borne in flat-topped clusters. The leaves are yellowish-green, and are deeply cut into almost fern-like proportions. Habitat: gardens, hedgerows, waste ground. Common throughout in suitable habitat.

Confusion plant: none.

Common Ragwort
Senecio jacobaea
Height: 30–150 cm
Flower: 1.5–2.5 cm, May–Nov
Tall and erect, often forming large patches; poisonous to animals. The yellow, daisy-like flowers occur in large, flat-topped clusters. Leaves are deeply lobed and toothed. Habitat: roadsides, neglected pastures, dunes and waste ground. Common throughout in suitable habitat.

Confusion plants: Hoary Ragwort, *Senecio erucifolius*, greyish with down; Marsh Ragwort, *Senecio aquaticus*, more branched, and larger flowers in bigger heads; Oxford Ragwort, *Senecio squalidus*, less lobed leaves, looser flower heads.

Groundsel
Senecio vulgaris
Height: 5–30 cm
Heads: 0.4–0.5 cm, Jan–Dec
A short but erect, branched, hairy plant. The yellow flowers are tiny and grow in shaving-brush-shaped heads. The leaves are lobed, irregularly toothed, and downy beneath. Habitat: waste ground, walls and rocky places. Common throughout in suitable habitat.

Confusion plant: none.

Lesser Burdock
Arctium minus
Height: 50–150 cm
Flower: 1.5–3 cm, Jul–Sep
Robust, downy-stemmed plant. Reddish-purple flowers in spherical heads which turn to prickly burs, attaching themselves to clothing and animal fur. Heart-shaped or oval leaves, downy texture; hollow leaf stems. Habitat: waste ground, hedges and woods. Common throughout in suitable habitat.

Confusion plant: Greater Burdock, *Arctium lappa*, has solid rather than hollow stalks, larger flowers (3–4 cm), and more rounded leaves.

Carline Thistle
Carlina vulgaris
Height: 15–60 cm
Flower: 1.5–4 cm, Jul–Oct
A relatively short thistle growing on stout, upright, branched stems. Flowers are yellowish-brown, always looking rather dried out. Narrowly oval and lobed leaves with spiny margins. Habitat: limestone-rich grassland. Uncommon, Rame Head is good.

    Confusion plant: none.

Musk Thistle (Nodding Thistle)
Carduus nutans
Height: 30–150 cm
Flower: 2–5 cm, Jun–Sep
An erect, slightly sprawling thistle with downy, white appearance and distinctive nodding heads. The reddish-purple flowers occur on solitary, nodding stalks. Each leaf has between six and ten pairs of spined lobes. Habitat: bare, sandy soils among grasses, most often coastal in Cornwall. Penhale is a good area. Widespread.

    Confusion plant: none.

Creeping Thistle
Cirsium arvense
Height: 50–150 cm
Flower: 1–2.5 cm, Jun–Sep
An erect, leafy-looking thistle with proportionately small flowers. Flowers pink and surrounded by dark bracts. Long and spear-shaped leaves with hairs and many spines. Habitat: waste ground, arable fields, pastures, woodlands, hedges. Extremely common.

    Confusion plant: none.

Common Thistle (Spear Thistle)

Cirsium vulgare
Height: 30–200 cm
Flower: 3–5 cm, Jul–Oct
A tall, erect, much-branched thistle with large flowers. Purple flowers with egg-shaped, almost globular body of spiny bracts; occur in clusters. Spear-shaped and deeply lobed leaves with very long spines; end lobe especially long and dangerous. Habitat: pastures, hedges, waste ground, disturbed ground. Common throughout in suitable habitat.

Confusion plant: none.

Common Knapweed (Hardheads)

Centaurea nigra
Height: 30–180 cm
Flower: 2–4 cm, Jun–Oct
A downy plant with much-branched stems. Flowers are pink and thistle-like, sometimes with extended rays; surrounded by scale-like bracts. Thin and oval leaves, becoming narrower further up stem. Habitat: any grasslands. Common throughout in suitable habitat.

Confusion plant: Greater Knapweed, *Centaurea scabiosa*, has lobed leaves and larger flowers (up to 5 cm across).

Sawwort

Serratula tinctoria
Height: 10–100 cm
Heads: 1.5–2 cm, Jul–Sep
Erect plant with strong, thin, branched stems; looks like a thistle but without spines. Pinkish-purple flowers are a little like knapweed, but less flamboyant. Leaves are lobed, and have a saw-toothed edge. Habitat: damp grassland. Uncommon.

Confusion plant: none.

Prickly Sow-thistle
Sonchus asper
Height: 30–120 cm
Flower: 2–2.5 cm, May–Nov
An erect, hairless, branched plant with greyish-green colouring. Pale yellow, dandelion-like flowers occurring in loose clusters. The leaves are arrow-shaped with spiny edges, firmly clasping the stem. Habitat: arable fields, waste ground and sandy soils. Common throughout in suitable habitat.

Confusion plant: Smooth Sow-thistle, *Sonchus oleraceus*, has greyer-green, less glossy leaves, with less sharp spines, and more deeply divided and lobed leaves.

Smooth Hawksbeard
Crepis capillaris
Height: 20–100 cm
Flower: 1–1.5 cm, Jun–Nov
A much-branched, dandelion-like plant; sparsely hairy. Flowers are yellow, with some reddish tinging, and occur in loose clusters. Leaves are deeply lobed. Habitat: grassland and waste ground. Common throughout in suitable habitat.

Confusion plants: other hawksbeards, hawkbits and catsears.

Common Catsear
Hypochaeris radicata
Height: 10–50 cm
Flower: 2.5–4 cm, May–Oct
A tufted plant with erect flower stems, has tiny bracts along its stems which can be felt by running fingers along the stem. Flowers are yellow and dandelion-like. Long leaves are roughly hairy and lobed. Habitat: grassland. This is the commonest of the dandelion-like flowers, of which there are many.

Confusion plants: several hawkbits, hawksbeards and hawkweeds are similar, but the tiny bracts along the stem help to identify the catsear.

Dandelion
Taraxacum officinale
Height: 50–40 cm
Flower: 2.5–4 cm, Feb–Nov
The flower stem, which is hollow with sap, grows from a basal rosette of leaves; the distinctive seedhead is known as a dandelion clock. The flowers are yellow, and consist entirely of ray florets. All the leaves occur at the base of the plant, and are variably lobed; hairless. Habitat: grassland and waste ground. Common throughout in suitable habitat.

Confusion plants: several dandelions, catsears, hawkbits, ox-tongues, hawksbeards and hawkweeds are similar in appearance: a specialist guide is needed to separate them all.

Bristly Oxtongue
Picris echioides
Height: 30–100 cm
Flower: 2–2.5 cm, Jun–Nov
An erect, much-branched plant covered with rough bristles. The flowers are dandelion-like but paler yellow, occurring in clusters. The leaves are oval and pointed, bristly, wavy edged, and show whitish pimples. Habitat: field margins, waste ground and grassland. Common throughout in suitable habitat.

Confusion plants: several dandelions, catsears, hawkbits, ox-tongues, hawksbeards and hawkweeds are similar in appearance: a specialist guide is needed to separate them all.

Snakeshead Fritillary
Fritillaria meleagris
Height: 10–30 cm
Flower: 3–5 cm, Apr–May
Each bulb has a single erect flowering stem which is hairless. Either white or purple flowers are tulip-shaped but nodding from one side of a slender stem. Narrow leaves grow from the stem. Habitat: grassland. Uncommon.

Confusion plant: none.

Bog Asphodel
Narthecium ossifragum
Height: 10–30 cm
Flower: 1–1.6 cm, Jun–Aug
A creeping plant with erect flower stems, which persist as brown stems long after the flowers have died. The flowers, which have six petals, are yellow and have orange stamens; they grow in spikes. The leaves are narrow and sword-shaped, all growing from the base of the flower stems. Habitat: bogs and wet heaths. Common throughout in suitable habitat.

Confusion plant: none.

Three-cornered Leek
Allium triquetrum
Height: 15–40 cm
Flower: 1.5–2.5 cm, Apr–May
Three-cornered stems hold a nodding head of flowers; strong garlic scent. White, bell-shaped flowers hang from the top of the stem in a single cluster. Linear leaves. Habitat: hedges, woodland and riversides. Common throughout in suitable habitat, a naturalized and invasive plant.

Confusion plant: Wild Garlic, *Allium ursinum*, has a similar scent, but has flowers in a hemispherical head and much broader leaves.

Wild Garlic (Ramsons)
Allium ursinum
Height: 15–40 cm
Flower: 0.8–1.2 cm, Apr–Jun
Each bulb has a single, erect flowering stem which is hairless; has a strong smell of garlic; grows in patches. White flowers have six petals in a star shape, in a hemispherical head at the top of a straight stem. Elliptical leaves grow from base of plant. Habitat: shady areas, particularly woodland. Common throughout in suitable habitat.

Confusion plant: Three-cornered Leek, *Allium triquetrum*, has bell-shaped flowers in nodding heads, and thinner leaves.

Bluebell (Wild Hyacinth)

Hyacinthoides non-scriptus
Height: 10–40 cm
Flower: 1–2 cm, Apr–May

A bulbous plant with erect stems, often carpeting the ground in woodland. Habitat: shady areas, particularly woodland. The flowers are violet-blue, sometimes white, and occur in a single-sided spike. The leaves are narrow and slightly fleshy, growing from the base. Habitat: mostly woodland, but also sea cliffs. Common throughout in suitable habitat.

Confusion plant: Spanish Bluebell, *Hyacinthoides his-panica*, is an invasive garden escape; it has broader leaves; a stouter stems, and flowers which grow from each side of the stem.

The world distribution of the bluebell is centred on Britain; in fact they are only found here and on the coastal fringe of north-western Europe. Across most of their range, bluebells occur only in woodlands, but because they enjoy the damp conditions in the South West it is possible to find them in coastal areas and even on cliff ledges, so long as the soil has remained undisturbed long enough for them to become established.

Being such a significant flower it isn't surprising that the bluebell has developed a range of common names, which include Culverkeys and Old Man's Bells. Superstition and folklore suggest that it has always been regarded as unlucky to bring its flowers into the house. It was once used to fulfil several purposes, including the production of glue for book-making and starch for stiffening collars.

Grape-hyacinth
Muscari neglectum
Height: 10–30 cm
Flower: 0.3–0.8 cm, Apr–May
A bulbous plant with erect flowers stems and basal leaves. The blue flowers are urn-shaped and occur in dense cylindrical heads. The leaves are narrow and rolled. Habitat: hedges, grassland and gardens. Common throughout in suitable habitat.

Confusion plant: Tassel-Hyacinth, *Muscari comosum*, has paler flowers with a white rim, and a looser flower spike with a 'tassel' of purple, sterile flowers at the top.

Spring Squill
Scilla verna
Height: 6–20 cm
Flower: 0.4–0.8 cm, Mar–Jun
A bulbous, fleshy plant with short, stout, erect stems and a basal rosette of leaves. The flowers are bluish-violet, occurring in a cluster, and all face upwards. The leaves are grass-like but fleshy, and often curving backwards. Habitat: grassland, particularly coastal. Common throughout in suitable habitat.

Confusion plant: Autumn Squill, *Scilla autumnalis*, flowers in late summer; has pyramidal-shaped flower clusters.

Black Bryony
Tamus communis
Height: 100–400 cm
Flower: 0.3–0.6 cm, May–Aug
A glossy, climbing plant, made obvious not by its flowers but its strings of red berries (see photo). The flowers are tiny and yellow-green, with six petals occurring in loose spikes. The leaves are glossy, dark green and heart-shaped. Habitat: hedges and woodland edges. Common throughout in suitable habitat.

Confusion plant: none.

Lords and Ladies (Cuckoo Pint)

Arum maculatum
Height: 20–40 cm
Spathe: Up to 25 cm, Apr–May
Distinctive flower shape in spring, and stout stem with red berries in autumn make this a very distinctive species. Club-shaped spike has small male flowers above females; this is surrounded by a sheath-like spathe. Arrow-shaped and basal leaves; light green and hairless. Habitat: woodland and hedges. Common throughout in suitable habitat.
Confusion plant: none.

The rhizome of this plant contains a great deal of starch, which was exploited in the Elizabethan Age to stiffen their ruffs, but it is the appearance of its flower which has attracted most attention. The erect, purple spadix contained within the embracing flower head has led to many fairly sordid local names, such as 'willy lily'. One of the more interesting names in quite common use is 'cuckoo pint', which at first might seem like an innocent reference to the time of its flowering and its ability to hold water, but alas no, the term pint is actually derived from an old German word for penis. It should come as no surprise to learn that the leaves of this plant were once used as an aphrodisiac.

Snowdrop

Galanthus nivalis
Height: 10–20 cm
Flower: 2–3 cm, Jan–Mar
A clump-forming, hairless plant. White, nodding flowers have three inner petals which are tipped green, and three outer petals. Chisel-tipped, long thin leaves all grow from the base. Habitat: woodlands, churchyards and gardens. Widespread.

Confusion plants: several varieties of snowdrop have been cultivated in gardens, otherwise can only possibly be confused with the Spring Snowflake, *Leucojum vernum*, which is much taller and has equal-lengthed petals.

The snowdrop chooses to climax at a very difficult time of year when, even in Cornwall, frosts can occur. Lying dormant underground as a bulb, it has the ability to emerge quickly at a time of year when most species have no choice but to wait. The chisel-like leaves are able to penetrate frosty ground, and a leaf-like structure protects the emerging flowers as they force their way through. Even with the ability to grow quickly snowdrops still need to be able to withstand the formation of ice inside their stems. Most plants would wilt and die in such conditions, but snowdrops are able to withdraw water from their cells and store it in voids, so that when it freezes it doesn't cause damage to the fragile cell structure.

Wild Daffodil
Narcissus pseudonarcissus
Height: 20–50 cm
Flower: 4–7 cm, Feb–Apl
A plant growing from a bulb, with erect flower stem and many leaves. The yellow flower has a trumpet-shaped corona and six petals which do not overlap as they do in cultivated varieties. The leaves are greyish-green and strap-like. Habitat: grassland and woodland. Uncommon because they have hybridized with introduced varieties; the Glynn Valley has some.

Confusion plant: cultivated varieties of daffodils.

Flag Iris
(Yellow Flag, Yellow Iris)
Iris pseudacorus
Height: 50–150 cm
Flower: 8–10 cm, May–Jul
A tall, stout plant forming clumps. Large yellow flowers are formed from three erect inner petals and three larger outer petals. Leaves are long and sword-shaped. Habitat: marshy ground. Common throughout in suitable habitat.

Confusion plant: Garden Iris, *Iris germanica*, is similar in size but with purple flowers.

Bee Orchid
Ophrys apifera
Height: 10–30 cm
Flower: 1–2 cm, Jun
An erect plant with tall, thin, often slightly twisting stem; surprisingly well camouflaged among grasses. The lower lip of the flower is bee-like in appearance; the outer sepals are pink; several flowers grow from different sides of each stem. The leaves are narrowly oval and unspotted. Habitat: grassland. Rare, found at Penlee Battery near Rame Head, and on a roundabout on the A30 near Hayle.

Confusion plant: none.

Early Purple Orchid
Orchis mascula
Height: 10–40 cm
Flower: 0.8–1.2 cm, Apr–May
An erect plant, with loose spike of flowers. Deep pink or purple flower with white centre; shapely flowers grow in a loose spike. Narrow, long and pointed leaves with purplish blotches. Habitat: woods, grassland and hedges. Common throughout in suitable habitat.

Confusion plants: most other pinkish orchids flower later in the season; the Green-winged Orchid, *Orchis morio*, can flower at the same time, but has green veins in its sepals, which form a hood over its flowers.

Green-winged Orchid
Orchis morio
Height: 10–40 cm
Flower: 0.7–1.2 cm, May–Jun
An erect plant with a short spike of loosely fitting flowers. Narrow, long and pointed, unspotted leaves. Habitat: dry rocky ground and grassland. Uncommon, one good location is the coastal grassland at Predannack on the Lizard.

Confusion plant: Early Purple Orchid, *Orchis mascula*, lacks green-veined hood and has spots on leaves.

Pyramidal Orchid
Anacamptis pyramidalis
Height: 10–40 cm
Flower: 0.6–0.8 cm, Jun–Jul
Erect, with tall, thin stem and distinctive flower spike. Pinkish-purple flowers, less ornately shaped than other similarly coloured orchids, occur in a dense flower spike which is the shape of an inverted cone in its early stages. Long, thin leaves are unspotted, mostly around base of the plant; some smaller leaves hug the stem. Frequent on dunes, occasionally other lime-rich grassland. Numerous only in restricted habitat types.

Confusion plants: other pink orchids with more tubular flower spikes much less common on dunes.

Heath Spotted Orchid
Dactylorhiza maculata
Height: 15–60 cm
Flower: 1.5–2 cm, Jun–Jul
Stout stem with flower spike; much smaller examples grow around the coast. Usually white or very pale pink flowers, with deeper pink patterning on petals; flowers occur in a dense flower spike. Leaves linear with brown spots; larger leaves at the base, but some from the stem. Habitat: moorland, heathland and some grassland. Fairly widespread in suitable habitat.

Confusion plant: paler than most other orchids; most easily confused with the Common Spotted Orchid, *Dactylorhiza fuchsii* (quite rare in Cornwall, restricted to grassland).

Southern Marsh Orchid
Dactylorhiza praetermissa
Height: 20–75 cm
Flower: 1.2–2.4 cm, May–Jul
Stout stem with flower spike, bracts often grow through the flowers. Pinkish flowers with darker spotting occur in a dense flower spike. Linear leaves, usually without spotting, occur on stem. Habitat: grassland, marshes, dune slacks. A relatively common orchid.

Confusion plant: Early Marsh Orchid, *Dactylorhiza incarnata*, also occurs in Cornwall, has less tightly packed flower spike, and can flower a little earlier in the year.

Fragrant Orchid
Gymnadenia conopsea
Height: 20–65 cm
Flower: 0.8–1 cm, Jun–Jul
Erect plant with tall, thin stem and loose flower spike. Deep pink and ornately shaped flowers form a loose flower spike which is scented. The leaves are narrow and unspotted. Habitat: marshy ground and dunes. Uncommon, good spots include Goonhilly Downs and Penhale Dunes (MOD area).

Confusion plant: other orchids, though fragrance is enough to clinch identification for certain.

Lesser Butterfly Orchid
Platanthera bifolia
Height: 20–40 cm
Flower: 0.6–1 cm, Jun

Erect plant with tall, thin stem topped by loose-fitting flower spike. Creamy white flower, very ornately shaped; lower lip is long with a greenish tinge; flower spike very loose; pollen sacks parallel. Large, oval leaves at base of stem; scale-like leaves on stem, no spotting. Habitat: grassland and heaths. Uncommon; Sylvia's Meadow is a good location.

Confusion plant: Greater Butterfly Orchid, *Platanthera chlorantha*, is less common; has pollen sacks at an angle; also at Sylvia's Meadow.

Common Twayblade
Listera ovata
Height: 20–60 cm
Flower: 1–1.5 cm, May–Jul

Erect plant with tall, thin leafless flower stem, a member of the orchid family. Flowers are green, with a long, narrow lower lip which has a deep notch cut into it; they are borne in tall, thin, loose spikes. There are two oval leaves at the base of the stem. Habitat: woodland, scrub and grassland. Uncommon.

Confusion plant: none in Cornwall.

Autumn Lady's Tresses
Spiranthes spiralis
Height: 5–30 cm
Flower: 0.5–1 cm, Aug–Sep

A short plant with slightly downy, erect flower spikes and a basal rosette of leaves. The flowers are white, and occur in a spiral fashion around a slightly twisted, slim flower spike. The basal leaves are pointed and oval; along the stem there are just a few small leaves. Habitat: dry grassland, particularly dunes. Uncommon.

Confusion plant: none.

Belladonna Lily (Naked Lady)

Amaryllis belladonna
Height: 40–70 cm
Flower: 5–10 cm, Aug–Nov

In spring the bulb grows leaves; in late summer or autumn it grows a flower stem. Several large pink flowers are carried at the top of a stout stem. The leaves are long and narrow. Habitat: old arable fields and hedges. An uncommon plant still grown commercially on the Scillies, found on the islands and in West Cornwall.

Confusion plant: none.

Agapanthus

Agapanthus praecox
Height: 50–120 cm
Flower: 2.6–5 cm, Jul–Oct

A tall, erect plant growing from a bulb, creating clumps. The funnel-shaped, blue flowers are carried in a large, spherical head (photo). The leaves are strap-like. Habitat: sandy soils. Only found naturalized in the Isles of Scilly, particularly the dunes of Tresco.

Confusion plant: none.

Hottentot Fig

Carpobrotus edulis
Height: Up to 400 cm
Flower: 5–10 cm, Apr–Aug

A sprawling, fleshy, hairless plant with long, slightly woody, trailing stems. The flowers can be yellow or pink. The leaves are extremely fleshy and heavy, with a triangular cross-section. Habitat: cliffs and beaches. Becoming more widespread, and is a threat to native coastal species.

Confusion plant: none.

Montbretia (Crocosmia)
Crocosmia crocosmiiflora(x)
Height: 30–100 cm
Flower: 2.4–3 cm, Jul–Sep
A hairless plant which produces extensive patches. The flowers are bright orange, and are carried in single-sided flower spikes. The pale green leaf is long and narrow. Habitat: hedges, waste ground and coastal areas. Widespread and common.

Confusion plant: the Wild Gladiolus, *Gladiolus illyricus*, often referred to as the 'Whistling Jack' is similar, but has reddish-purple flowers and a more erect flower spike.

Japanese Knotweed
Fallopia japonica
Height: Up to 300 cm
Flower: Tiny, Aug–Oct
A robust plant with cane-like, hollow stems; forms extensive patches. The small white flowers grow in large, frothy clusters. The leaves are large and heart-shaped. Habitat: waste ground, riversides and road verges. This is an extremely invasive plant and is widespread.

Confusion plant: none.

Himalayan Balsam (Indian Balsam)
Impatiens glandulifera
Height: 100–200 cm
Flower: 2.5–4 cm, Jul–Oct
A stout, hairless plant with hollow, ridged stems. The flower is pink or white, forming the shape of a large sac with petals at the front. The leaves are spear-shaped and have reddish margins. Habitat: mostly along rivers. A very invasive weed which uses rivers to spread its seed after ejecting them using a very effective twisting seedpod mechanism.

Confusion plant: none.

Fuchsia

Fuchsia magellanica
Height: Up to 300 cm
Flower: Up to 4 cm, Jul–Oct
A shrubby plant with woody stems. The flowers are bell-shaped, and combine red and purple. The leaves are oval and toothed. Habitat: hedges and gardens. Originally introduced as a hedging plant, it is not considered particularly invasive.

Confusion plant: none.

Glossary

Throughout this book I have tried to restrict the use of specialist words. A few that I have used that might not be familiar to everyone include the following:

- **Disc Florets** are most easily thought of as the central, yellow disc shape of a daisy flower.
- **Ray Florets** can also be found on a daisy. but are the white outer petals.
- **Sepals** are the structures behind the petals, and are usually, but not always, less colourful.
- The term **calyx** is used when the sepals are joined: for example, the Cowslip has a 'calyx tube'.
- **Bracts** are like leaves, situated just behind the flower. These are particularly obvious in the thistle family, where the head of the flower is largely made up of scale-like bracts.
- The word **linear** is often used to describe a leaf which has parallel sides.
- If leaves **alternate** then they do not grow opposite each other.

- If a leaf is **lobed** then it is deeply toothed, but not to the point of one leaf appearing as several leaflets.
- A **stamen** is the male part of the plant which is often obvious because it consists of the pollen sac held out from the flower on a filament.

Western gorse and heather on Nanjulian cliff

Some Top Spots for Wildflowers

There are some very special places for wildflowers in Cornwall, and those that are mentioned in the text are detailed below. Places are listed alphabetically, with grid reference, location, habitat and, sometimes, special flowers that can be seen there.

Note:
- CCC – Cornwall County Council
- CWT – Cornwall Wildlife Trust
- MOD – Ministry of Defence
- NE – Natural England
- NT – National Trust

Bissoe Valley, SW 769 415, contains some ponds on a CWT reserve

Boscregan Farm, SW 360 298, is a NT farm with some unusual arable weeds

Caerthillian Cove, SW 694 124, is on the Lizard

Cotehele, SX 424 682, is a house and estate owned by the NT near Calstock

Enys, SW 792 365, is a privately owned garden near Penryn renowned for its bluebells, open on just a couple of days per week. Tel 01872 274536 for more details

Glynn Valley is a heavily wooded part of the county alongside the main railwayline between Bodmin and Plymouth

Godrevy, SW 581 433, is near Hayle

Goonhilly Downs is a heathland owned by NE with free access from a car-park at SW 729 212

Hayle roundabout, SW 543 362, is a good spot for Bee Orchids, on the A30 at the Lelant junction

Kit Hill, SX 375 714, is owned by CCC

Kynance Cove, SW 688 133, is on the Lizard peninsula

Newlyn Downs, SW 835 545, is an area of heath near St Newlyn East

Penhale Sands is an area of dunes part-owned by CCC, part by a holiday camp, and part by the MOD. The centre of the dunes is at approximately SW 767 564.

Penlee Battery, SX 439 491, is a CWT reserve near Rame Head

Polly Joke, SW 772 606, is near Crantock

Predannack, SW 660 163, is an area of coastal heath near Mullion on the Lizard

Rame Head, SX 422 487, is near Torpoint

Sylvia's Meadow, SX 413 707, is a CWT reserve near Callington, with limited access

West Pentire, SW 776 606, is an area of arable fields with an exceptional show of arable weeds in late June and July. It is owned by the NT

Index of Wildflowers

This index lists all the wildflowers mentioned in the text. Species are listed alphabetically by common name and page number in the book. Entries in pink type denote species that are aliens; those in blue are highlighted species, and those in green do not have photographs. That in small capitals is an alien and has no photograph.

Organizations and Groups

Cornwall County Council,
Environment & Heritage Section
Cornwall County Council, Old County Hall,
Truro TR1 3AY
Tel: 01872 222 000
www.cornwall.gov.uk

Cornwall Wildlife Trust
Five Acres, Allet, nr Truro TR4 9DJ
Tel: 01872 273 939
www.cornwallwildlifetrust.org.uk

  Note: The Botanical Cornwall Group has
many workshops and field meetings suitable
for people with an interest in flowers, their
website is www.floracam.co.uk/bcg

Isles of Scilly Wildlife Trust
Carn Thomas, St Mary's,
Isles of Scilly TR21 0PT
Tel: 01720 422 153
www.ios-wildlifetrust.org.uk

National Trust, Cornwall Office
Lanhydrock, Bodmin PL30 4DE
Tel: 01208 742 81
www.nationaltrust.org.uk

**Natural England, Cornwall &
Isles of Scilly Team**
Trevint House, Strangways Villas,
Truro TR1 2PA
Tel: 01872 265 710,
head office 01733 455 000
www.naturalengland.org.uk